Building enduring customer relationships through sales execution and service is critical to our success. Congratulations, you have achieved the Circle of Excellence and the opportunity to enjoy a sales rally in Nashville! It's an entertaining place to visit, full of life and character, captured brilliantly in the pages ahead.

We hope your days in Music City have been memorable. Please accept this collection of city images as a small token of our appreciation for your diligent commitment and dedication. We look forward to your continued success!

Sincerely,

Mary Navarro   Jim Baron   Jim Lockhart   Rob Comfort   Belinda Sherman

NASHVILLE
TENNESSEE

A PHOTOGRAPHIC PORTRAIT

PHOTOGRAPHY BY DAVID BAILEY

NARRATIVE BY JOE MORRIS

Copyright © 2010 by
Twin Lights Publishers, Inc.

All rights reserved. No part of this book may be reproduced in any form without written permission of the copyright owners. All images in this book have been reproduced with the knowledge and prior consent of the artists concerned and no responsibility is accepted by producer, publisher, or printer for any infringement of copyright or otherwise, arising from the contents of this publication. Every effort has been made to ensure that credits accurately comply with information supplied.

First published in the United States of America by:

Twin Lights Publishers, Inc.
8 Hale Street
Rockport, Massachusetts 01966
Telephone: (978) 546-7398
http://www.twinlightspub.com

ISBN: 978-1-934907-01-6
ISBN: 1-934907-01-4

10 9 8 7 6 5 4 3 2 1

(*opposite*)
Nashville Skyline

(*frontispiece*)
Belle Mead Plantation House

(*jacket front*)
General Jackson

Book design by:
SYP Design & Production, Inc.
www.sypdesign.com

Printed in China

Nashville, Tennessee is a city flavored with history, culture, and beauty. More than 200 years ago, settlers established Fort Nashborough along the banks of the Cumberland River. Within a decade, the settlement grew with general stores, schools, and taverns, and underwent a name change to become Nashville. Echoes of an earlier American way of living can almost be heard throughout the city's antebellum mansions, where modern-day life seems to melt away on a sultry, summer afternoon. Nashville's rich past has helped to mold it into the vibrant city it is today. In the evening, "Music City U.S.A." comes alive in the nightclubs and honky-tonks of Lower Broadway, where many country-music legends got their start and where tomorrow's stars continue to be heard today.

Visitors to Nashville marvel over the city's dual nature, and no wonder. Here you can find an 1800s mansion not too far from a bustling, modern turnpike, as well as a full-scale reproduction of Athens, Greece's Parthenon. The past is never too far removed from the present, fitting for a city that saw its share of bloodshed during the Civil War. Nashville honors that history while also working through its many institutions of higher learning to promote peace and justice both at home and around the world.

Education is a major focus in Nashville, from well-known halls of higher learning such as Vanderbilt University and Fisk University, to cutting-edge research in the health-care industry. Museums such as the Frist Center for the Visual Arts, along with other art and education centers, round out the city's many cultural offerings.

Nashville's architecture is a contrast of old and new, reflecting a rich past and sophisticated future. However, the city's heart and soul is its people and its music. The country-music capital of the world boasts such institutions as the Grand Ole Opry that beams the Nashville sound around the globe every week. Plenty of other musical styles flourished here in Nashville as well, a fact evidenced by the beautiful Schermerhorn Symphony Center, a venue influenced by the grand concert halls of Europe with its central hall, plaza, and fountains.

In addition to the exciting urban landscape, the beautiful rolling hills of Middle Tennessee, along with parks, lakes, and trails, are all part of what makes Nashville so unique. Working farms and vineyards offer up the fruits of the land, and tantalize the senses.

With a proud hand on a rich past and a keen eye on a bright future, Nashville, the "Athens of the South," continues to offer an exceptional quality of life to those who visit and to those who call her home. Photographer David Bailey invites you to come and walk down Adelicia Acklen's staircase, enjoy the views from atop Fort Negley, cheer for the team at a Tennessee Titans game, or listen in on music legends at the Country Music Hall of Fame and Museum. This beautiful photographic journal will have you visiting Nashville again and again.

Music Row (opposite)

Ten-foot-tall fiberglass Gibson model guitars, placed all around the city, were part of Nashville's Guitar Town Project. Businesses donated to several local charities to host each guitar, and then the colorful instruments of art were sold at auction. The project was administered through the Gibson Foundation.

World War II Memorial

Bicentennial Mall State Park was created for the state's 200th birthday in 1996. The 19-acre park features many unique memorials, including this 18,000-pound granite globe commemorating World War II. The globe floats on one-eighth-inch of water, can be turned by hand, and shows the mileage from Tennessee to the war's major theaters.

96th Answer Bell

Located on the grounds of the Tennessee State Capitol, just above Bicentennial Mall State Park, the 96th Answer Bell rings out in retort to its 95 cousins located on the mall below, symbolizing a government answering to its people. The carillons are among the largest in the world.

Carillions and Court of 3 Stars
(above and opposite)

Constructed of red, white, and blue granite, the Court of 3 Stars anchors the northern end of Bicentennial Mall State Park. The three colors are representative of the three Grand Divisions of the state – East, Middle, and West. The court is also home to a 95-bell carillon, which reflects Tennessee's musical heritage.

Legislative Plaza

The Tennessee Legislative Plaza and walkways connect the state capitol building to the rest of downtown Nashville. In addition to legislative offices, the plaza is home to the War Memorial Auditorium and many statues and plaques commemorating the state's contributions during wartime, as well as other historic events in the nation's history.

War Memorial

The Nashville War Memorial Auditorium is overseen by the Tennessee Performing Arts Center and is used for concerts, performances, and other public events. The 1,600-seat auditorium and its plaza sit on the west side of the Tennessee Legislative Plaza. This historic landmark also houses the state's military history museum.

Andrew Jackson Statue (opposite)

President Andrew "Old Hickory" Jackson exercised great military prowess at the Battle of New Orleans during the War of 1812. His leadership is commemorated with this statue, located on the grounds of the Tennessee State Capitol building. Jackson was one of three Tennesseans elected to the presidency.

Andrew Jackson Gravesite (above)

President Andrew Jackson erected this tomb in honor of his wife, Rachel, who died in 1828 just before he took office. He is buried alongside her, under the canopy found in the corner of Rachel's beloved garden at the Hermitage, Jackson's home.

Nashville City Cemetery *(top and bottom)*

Nashville City Cemetery, one of the city's oldest cemeteries, was established in 1822. A few notables buried here are a state governor, four Confederate generals, some 15 Nashville mayors, and Samuel Read Anderson, who named the American flag "Old Glory." The cemetery is on the National Register of Historic Places.

Pathway of History

The west side of Bicentennial Mall State Park features a 1,400-foot Wall of History. Engraved with historic events, which have occurred over Tennessee's two centuries of statehood, the wall breaks at the time of the Civil War to symbolize how the state's citizens were split during the conflict.

State Capitol (above)

Tennessee's state capitol building, opened in 1859, is one of the longest continually operating capitol facilities in the nation. Architect William Strickland considered it his crowning achievement. Strickland requested that upon his death, which occured in 1854, he be buried in the building's north façade.

Senator Edward Ward Carmack (opposite)

A leader in the state's temperance movement, Senator Edward Ward Carmack championed many causes during his lifetime. During the early 1900s, and afterward as a newspaper editor, he pushed for prohibition. He was killed in 1908, in an accident that some anti-liquor activists have labeled an assassination.

Tomb of President and Mrs. James K. Polk

President and Mrs. James K. Polk's tomb is located on the grounds of the Tennessee State Capitol building. During his presidency, from 1845 to 1849, Polk secured the Oregon Territory, and oversaw both the opening of the Smithsonian Institution and the early stages of constructing the Washington Monument. He was also the first U.S. president to not seek re-election.

Davidson County Courthouse *(opposite, top)*

The Davidson County Courthouse has been the administrative seat for the city of Nashville and the surrounding county since they unified their governments in 1963. It was dedicated in December 1937 and has been the site of multiple noteworthy events, including Civil Rights demonstrations. It recently re-opened after a multimillion-dollar restoration and renovation effort.

Downtown Library *(opposite, bottom)*

The Downtown Library is the hub of Nashville's innovative, progressive library system. The 51-million dollar, 300,000-square-foot facility opened in June 2001, and features a marionette theatre, expansive oral-history archives, central courtyard, Civil Rights Room, and more than 500,000 books, periodicals, and audio-visual materials.

19

Governor's Mansion *(above and opposite)*

The Tennessee executive residence, originally named "Far Hills," was built for the William Ridley Wills family in 1929. It became the state's third governor's mansion when it was purchased in 1949. It has been the home to eight governors and has hosted presidents, celebrities, and royalty from around the globe.

Downtown Presbyterian Church *(above)*

Designed by architect William Strickland, who designed the state's capitol building as well, Downtown Presbyterian Church was completed in 1851. Strickland's use of the Egyptian Revival style made the Church's sanctuary beautiful and unique. The building is one of only a handful of similar churches left standing in the United States.

Customs House *(opposite)*

Construction of the Federal Building/Customs House began in 1877 with President Rutherford B. Hayes laying the cornerstone. His was the first visit by a sitting president since the end of the Civil War. The Customs House opened in 1882 and housed the city's post office, federal Treasury Department offices, as well as the Justice Department offices and courtrooms.

Athena (opposite)

Athena Parthenos, by sculptor Alan LeQuire, is a full-scale replica of a statue that graced the original Parthenon in Athens, Greece. She stands almost 42 feet tall and weighs 12 tons. In 2002 she was painted and received gold gilding. For perspective, the statue of *Nike* in her hand is 6 feet 4 inches tall.

Parthenon (above)

At the center of Centennial Park stands the Parthenon, an exact-size replica of the original in Athens, Greece. It was built in 1897 as part of the Tennessee Centennial Exposition, and reflects Nashville's reputation as the "Athens of the South." The original, made of plaster, wood, and brick, was replaced by the current concrete structure in the 1920s.

Natchez Trace Parkway Bridge (top)

The Natchez Trace Parkway Bridge is a double-arch, concrete bridge in Williamson County, near the parkway's northern terminus. The bridge's unique construction concentrates its weight at the crown of its arch. Completed in October 1993, it is the first segmentally-constructed concrete arch bridge in the United States.

Riverfront Park (bottom)

Nashville's Riverfront Park is a favorite spot with benches and walkways that allow for relaxing riverside afternoons. The park's permanent and temporary stages play host to many concerts and events, most notably the concert by the Nashville Symphony Orchestra and the city's legendary fireworks display.

Percy Warner Park

Percy Warner Park and Edwin Warner Park together comprise the largest municipally-administered park areas in Tennessee. The area covers 2,684 acres. Both parks opened in 1927 and are listed on the National Register of Historic Places. More than 500,000 people visit annually to enjoy hiking, golfing, horseback riding, and picnicking.

Edwin Warner Park *(above and opposite)*

The Warner Park Nature Center is found in Edwin Warner Park, and includes a museum of local natural history, a library, as well as an organic vegetable and herb garden, beehives, and wildflower garden. The Nature Center offers interpretive literature of the grounds and maps of the park's nature trails.

Middle Tennessee's lush flora and fauna are on vivid display throughout Edwin Warner Park and its twin, Percy Warner Park. The quiet retreats become livelier every spring, when the two parks host the Iroquois Steeplechase, a fixture on the local social calendar since May of 1941.

Grape Harvesting

Arrington Vineyards turns its lucious grapes into high-quality wines. The winery won "Best of Show" for its Syrah at the Wines of the South competition. Hailed as a first-class operation, Arrington continues to grow and expand both its vineyards and its national product-distribution network.

Arrington Vineyards

Arrington Vineyards was launched in 2005 by country artist Kix Brooks (half of famed duo Brooks & Dunn), businessman Fred Mindermann, and winemaker Kip Summers. In 2007, the winery building itself was finished and the first vintage was bottled. The vineyard is visited by tourists and wine aficionados alike.

Jack Daniel's Distillery

The Jack Daniel's Distillery received its license in 1866, making it the oldest registered distillery in the United States. Visitors from all over the world come to this Lynchburg landmark, which offers tours of the distillery and grounds, along with a liberal dose of lore regarding founder Jasper Newton "Jack" Daniel.

Jack Daniel's Warehouse

Jack Daniel's Tennessee Whiskey, a special category as per the U.S. government, is made with local spring water prized for its lack of iron. It is filtered through sugar-maple charcoal and stored in large wooden barrels where it ages in the warehouses that dot the distillery's property.

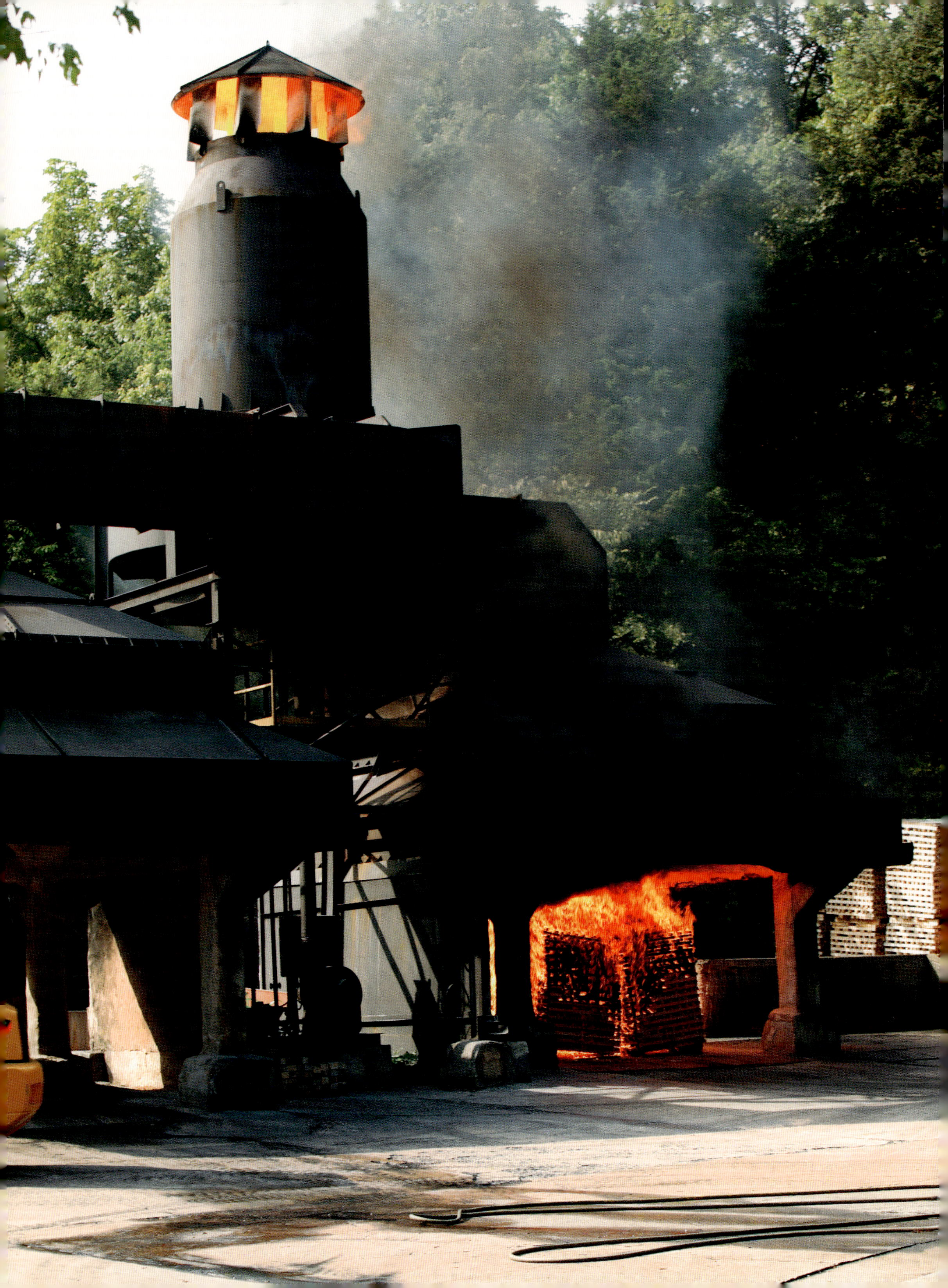

Jack Daniel's Rickyard *(opposite)*

The rickyard at Jack Daniel's produces the ground charcoal placed in the huge mellowing tanks that hold the whiskey during the distillery's legendary charcoal-mellowing process. The 140-proof whiskey seeps very slowly through 10 feet of charcoal, which removes the bad-tasting oils present in any grain alcohol.

Jack Daniel's Barrels *(above)*

When the 12-day mellowing process is complete, Jack Daniel's whiskey is placed into new, charred, white-oak barrels for aging. These containers are then stacked in "barrel houses," where they expand and contract with the changing seasonal temperatures, forcing the whiskey in and out of the wood, which gives it a rich amber color.

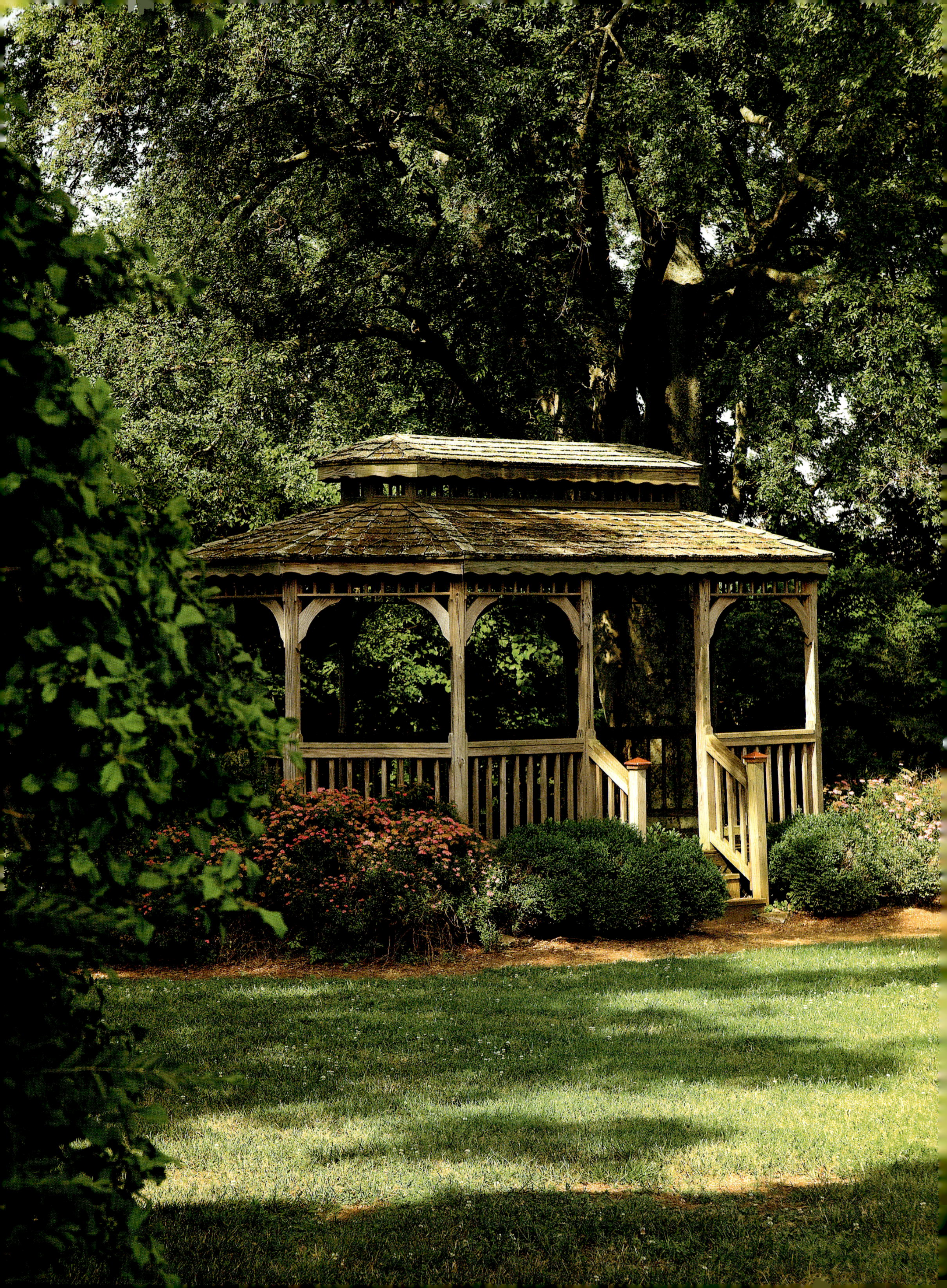

Wedding Gazebo *(opposite)*

The grounds at Two Rivers Mansion reflect the home's antebellum history, offering hidden nooks and cozy spots full of ambiance for visitors to discover and enjoy year-round. The estate and gardens continue to be a popular spot for weddings, reunions, and many other public and private functions.

Two Rivers Mansion *(above)*

Construction on the Italianate-style Two Rivers Mansion began in 1859, and was completed just before the outbreak of the Civil War. Built by David and Willie McGavock, the impressive home lies between the Stones and Cumberland rivers. Since 1965, the mansion and grounds have been owned by the city of Nashville.

Bygone Days

Outbuildings played an integral part in the operation of larger homes such as Two Rivers Mansion. These smaller structures served many vital functions for the larger, main property such as offices, kitchens, slave quarters, or smokehouses. They typically encircled the rear of the dominant home.

Delightful Cherub

The statuary and outdoor ornamentation at Two Rivers Mansion attribute to the extensive detail that went into the making of this magnificent home. Built in the Italianate style, the mansion's gardens are an important part of its overall elegance. A walk around the gardens is truly a trip back to a bygone era.

Travellers Rest *(top and bottom)*

Travellers Rest Historic House Museum replicates life in Middle Tennessee from the Native American period through the Civil War, with a focus on the period from 1789 to 1833. The home and grounds are held in trust by the National Society of the Colonial Dames of America in Tennessee.

Nashville's antebellum and historical homes and gardens not only showcase period houses, but also how residents lived and worked during that time. Re-enactors at Travellers Rest Historic House Museum and other estates are period-perfect representations, giving visitors a living, breathing glimpse back in time.

Mansker's Station (top and bottom)

The fort, built in 1779 by Kasper Mansker and other settlers, draws history buffs to Goodlettsville. Here they can experience the life of an 18th-century settler at Mansker's Station, as well as the historic Bowen Plantation house, the oldest brick house in Middle Tennessee.

The Hermitage

President Andrew Jackson built The Hermitage, a Greek Revival-style mansion, in 1819 for himself and his wife, Rachel. Following his two terms as president in 1837, Jackson retired to The Hermitage and lived there quietly until his death in 1845. Both he and Rachel are buried in the gardens.

The Hermitage

President Jackson always enjoyed company, so it seems fitting that The Hermitage has had more than 15 million visitors since it opened as a museum in 1889. The home is adorned with period furnishings from 1837, the year Jackson returned following his second term as president.

Cheekwood Botanical Garden *(top and bottom)*

The Cheekwood mansion attributes to the financial savvy of one of Nashville's most successful business families. The Cheek family created Maxwell House coffee, marketed through and named for a fine local hotel. The brand's sale led to the purchase of 100 acres and construction of the home, which was completed in 1932.

When the Cheeks built their west Nashville mansion, they wanted the rolling, expansive grounds around it to enhance the beauty of their home. With that in mind, landscape architect Bryant Fleming oversaw the installation of formal gardens, designed in minute detail to reflect English gardens of the 18th century.

Cheekwood Botanical Garden and Museum

Members of the Cheek family lived at Cheekwood until the 1950s, when they allowed it to become a botanical garden and art museum. The Nashville Museum of Art donated its permanent collection, while the Exchange Club of Nashville, the Horticultural Society of Middle Tennessee, and other civic groups redeveloped the property.

Carter House

The Federal-style brick home was built by Fountain Branch Carter between 1828 and 1830. The house survived the horrific Battle of Franklin in 1864 and its exterior still sports more than 1,000 bullet holes from the gunfire that took place around it. The Carter House is located in the middle of downtown Franklin.

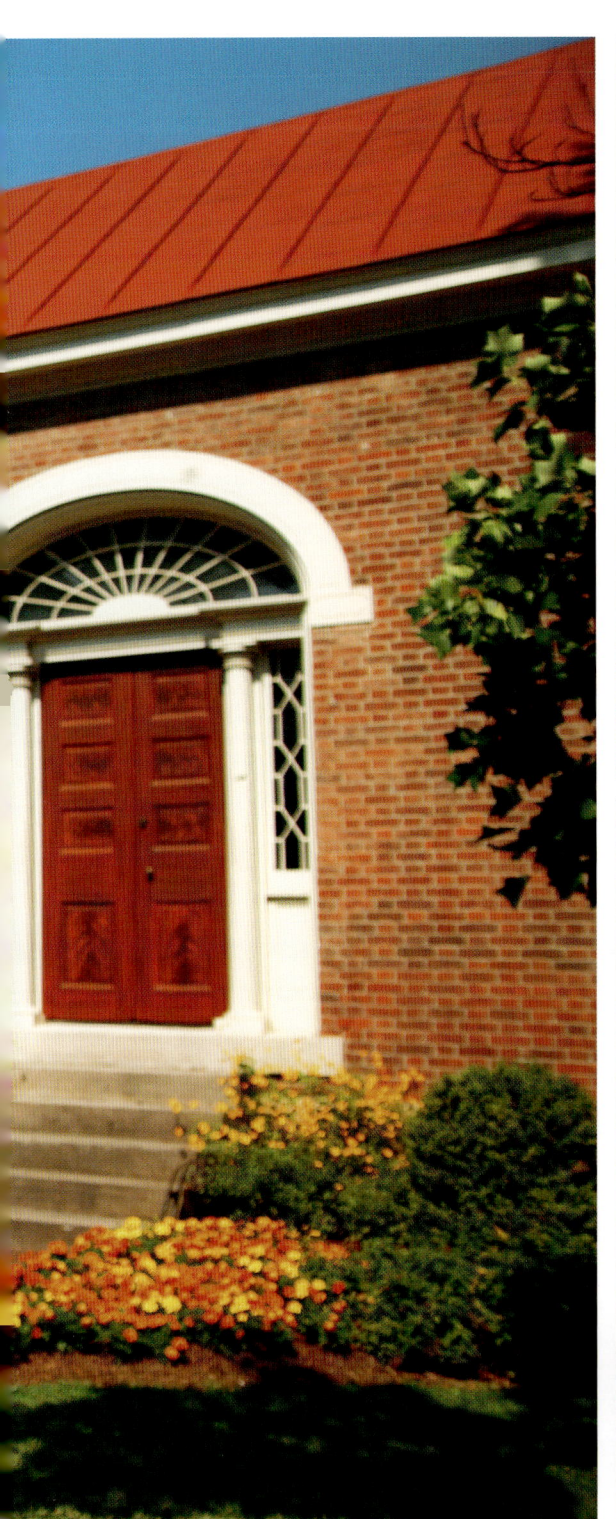

Carter House *(top and bottom)*

The Carter House, like most buildings of its era, was surrounded with outbuildings, such as the farm office, smokehouse, and kitchen, which contributed to the operation of the home and farm. Like the main house, the outbuildings are pockmarked with bullet holes that give mute evidence of the horrors of war.

The only battles near the Carter House these days are for parking, but this cannon and other weaponry on the grounds remind visitors of the home's unwilling role as bystander during the Battle of Franklin. The nearby battlefield and cemetery also are reminders of that dark Civil War day.

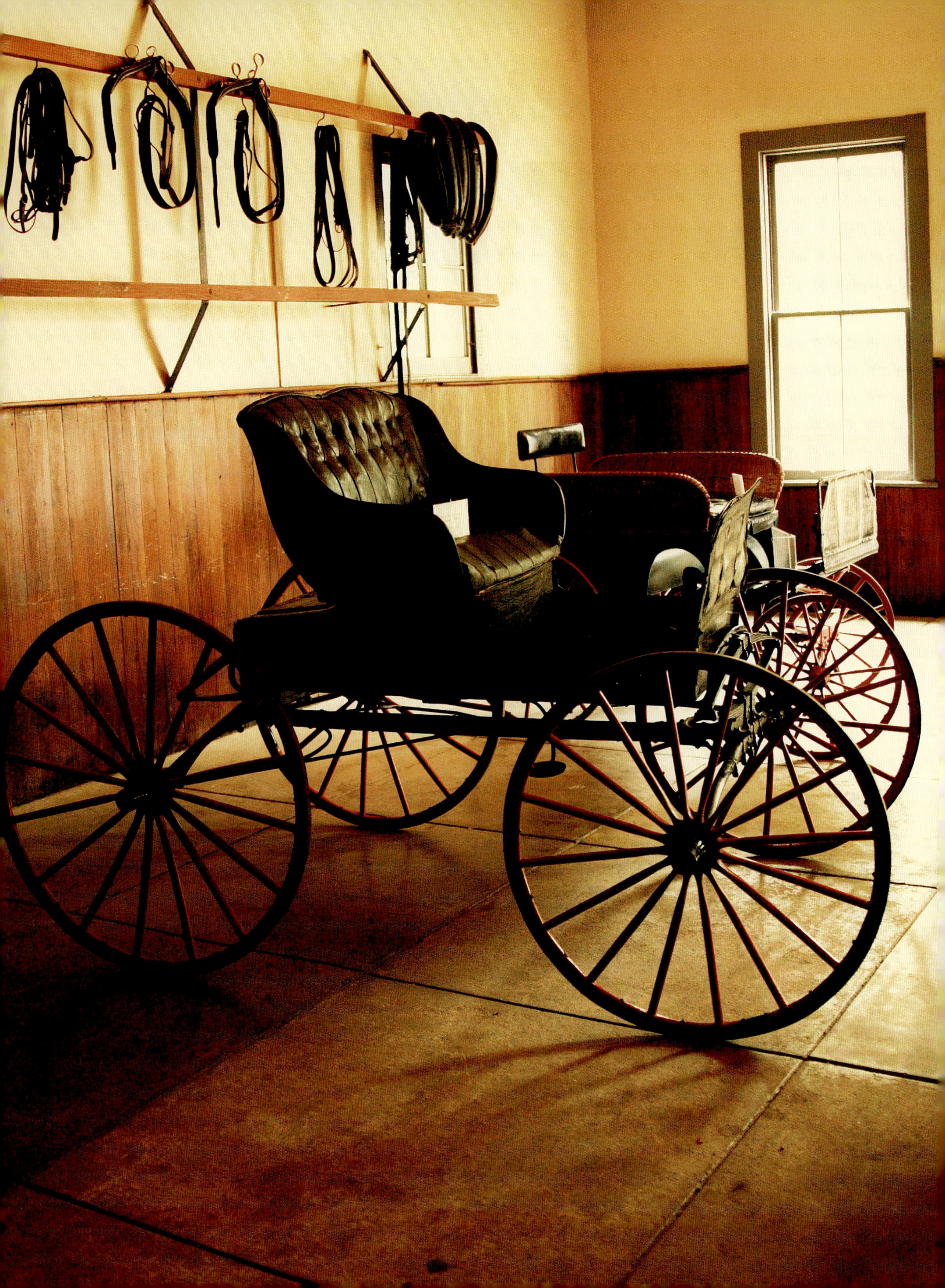

Belle Mead Plantation *(opposite and above)*

For more than 200 years, Belle Meade Plantation has been at the epicenter of Nashville's equestrian circles. While the estate now is a tourist destination, its legendary history as a thoroughbred breeding site is reflected in this carriage, one of many historical conveyances found on the property.

The carriage house and stables at Belle Meade Plantation were built in 1892, and operated for decades boarding and breeding thoroughbred horses. The Association for the Preservation of Tennessee's Antiquities now operates the site as a museum.

Carnton Plantation

Built in 1826, Carnton Plantation served as a field hospital during the Battle of Franklin. Recently, the home and its mistress, Carrie McGavock, were the inspiration for a best-selling fictional account by local author Robert Hicks called *The Widow of the South*.

Confederate Cemetery *(top and bottom)*

The McGavock Confederate Cemetery is adjacent to the Carnton Plantation. The two-acre plot was set aside by John and Carrie McGavock in 1866 as a burial place for approximately 1,500 Confederate soldiers. It was maintained by the couple until their deaths. The cemetery now is the largest privately-owned military cemetery in the nation.

Rolling Farmland

Today, the serene, rolling farmland surrounding Carnton Plantation gives little evidence that it was the site of one of the Civil War's bloodiest skirmishes. The Battle of Franklin took place on November 30, 1864, where, over the course of five hours, more than 1,700 Confederate soldiers were killed.

Carnton Plantation

Carnton Plantation was owned by the McGavock family until 1911. In 1973, after much local lobbying, Carnton and 30 adjacent acres were listed on the National Register of Historic Places. In 1977, the badly neglected house and 10 acres were donated to the Carnton Association, which has carefully restored the landmark site.

Belmont Mansion *(left, above, and opposite)*

The eternally stylish and elegant Belmont Mansion remains a tribute to its mistress, Adelicia Hayes Franklin Acklen Cheatham. Born in 1817, she was left wealthy and widowed at a young age. She and later husband, Joseph Acklen, completed the lavish 36-room, Italianate-style home in 1853 on what are now the grounds of Belmont University.

Following the Civil War, Mrs. Acklen and her children traveled through Europe, where she collected marble statuary and other large-scale art for her growing collection. The grounds of Belmont Mansion contain some of her treasures, as well as the largest collection of 19th-century, cast-iron garden ornaments in the United States.

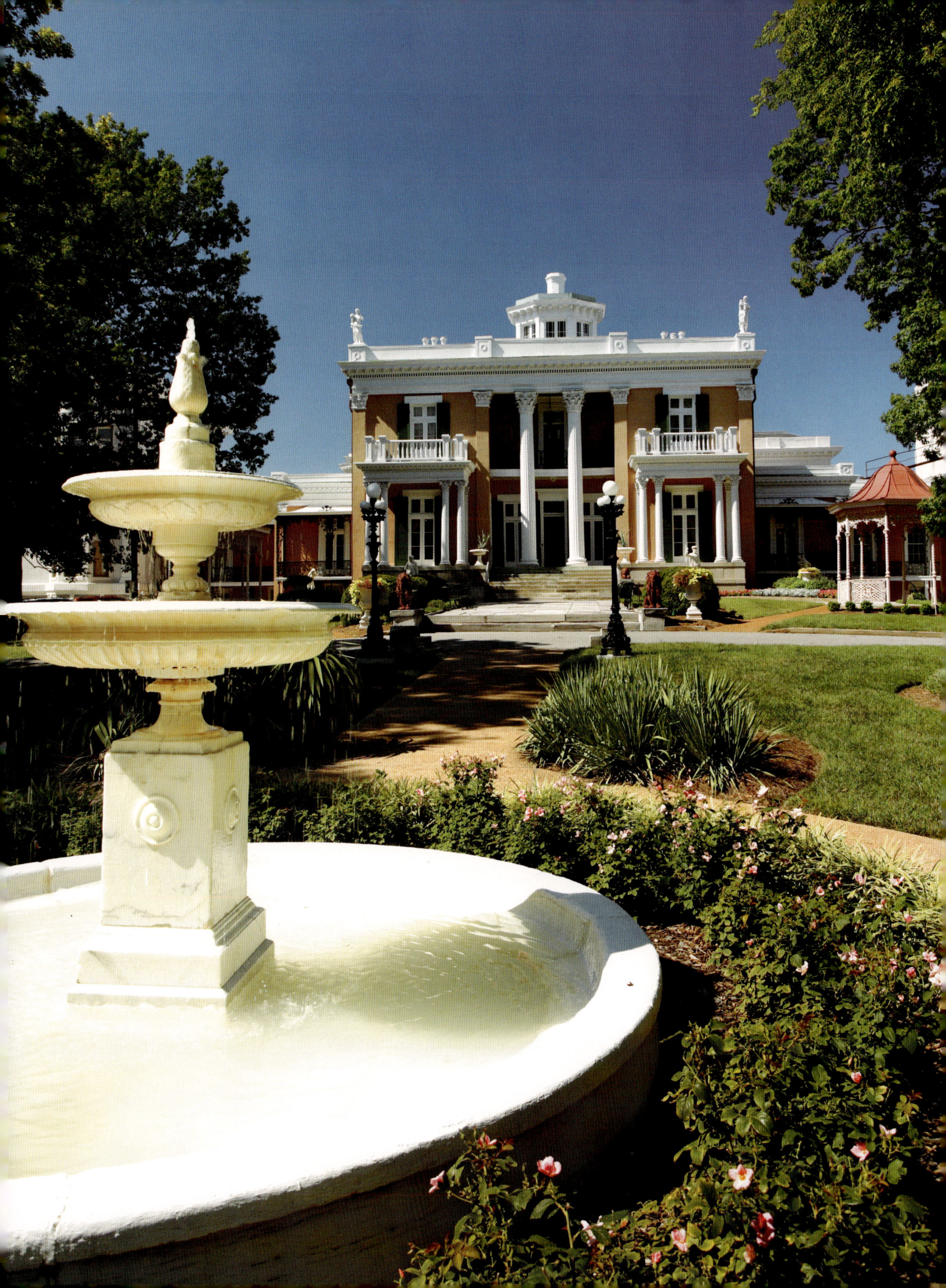

Fort Nashboro *(above and opposite)*

In the shadow of downtown's skyscrapers, this recreation of Fort Nashborough on the bluff, overlooking the Cumberland River, shows how the area's earliest settlers lived and worked. Built in 1962, the five log cabins and the fort compound itself offers visitors an authentic sense of frontier life during 1779.

Nashville's earliest settlers were plagued by attacks from the area's Indian population, some of whom did not recognize their claims to the territory. These attacks continued for years, but eventually, political winds shifted within the tribes, allowing the area's first citizens to make peace with the land's original caretakers.

JOHN DONELSON
THE FOUNDING OF NASHVILLE
Thomas Puryear Mims
Sculptor

Fort Negley Visitors Center *(top)*

The Fort Negley Visitors Center is a modern-day time machine, taking history buffs back to 1862 and the Fall of Nashville. Multimedia presentations show how that battle transformed the city into one of the Union's major supply depots for the Western Theater for the duration of the Civil War.

Fort Negley *(bottom)*

From its location high above the city, Fort Negley stands as a monument to the 2,768 free African-Americans and slaves who built it on behalf of the Union. The workmen paid a heavy price, with between 600 and 800 dying during construction of the four-acre fort. Only 310 ever received any pay.

Sally Ports (above)

Sally ports were used by Union troops to enter into Fort Negley, enabling them to look down upon the city's land and water entrance and exit points. The installation was the largest inland masonry fort built during the Civil War, and was 600 feet long by 300 feet wide.

General Jackson Showboat (pages 60–61)

Measuring 300 feet long, the *General Jackson* showboat is one of the largest paddlewheel riverboats in the United States. It has four decks surrounding its Victorian theater, where lavish musical shows are performed. The ship can hold 1,200 passengers and sails from the Gaylord Opryland Resort & Convention Center to cruise along the Cumberland River.

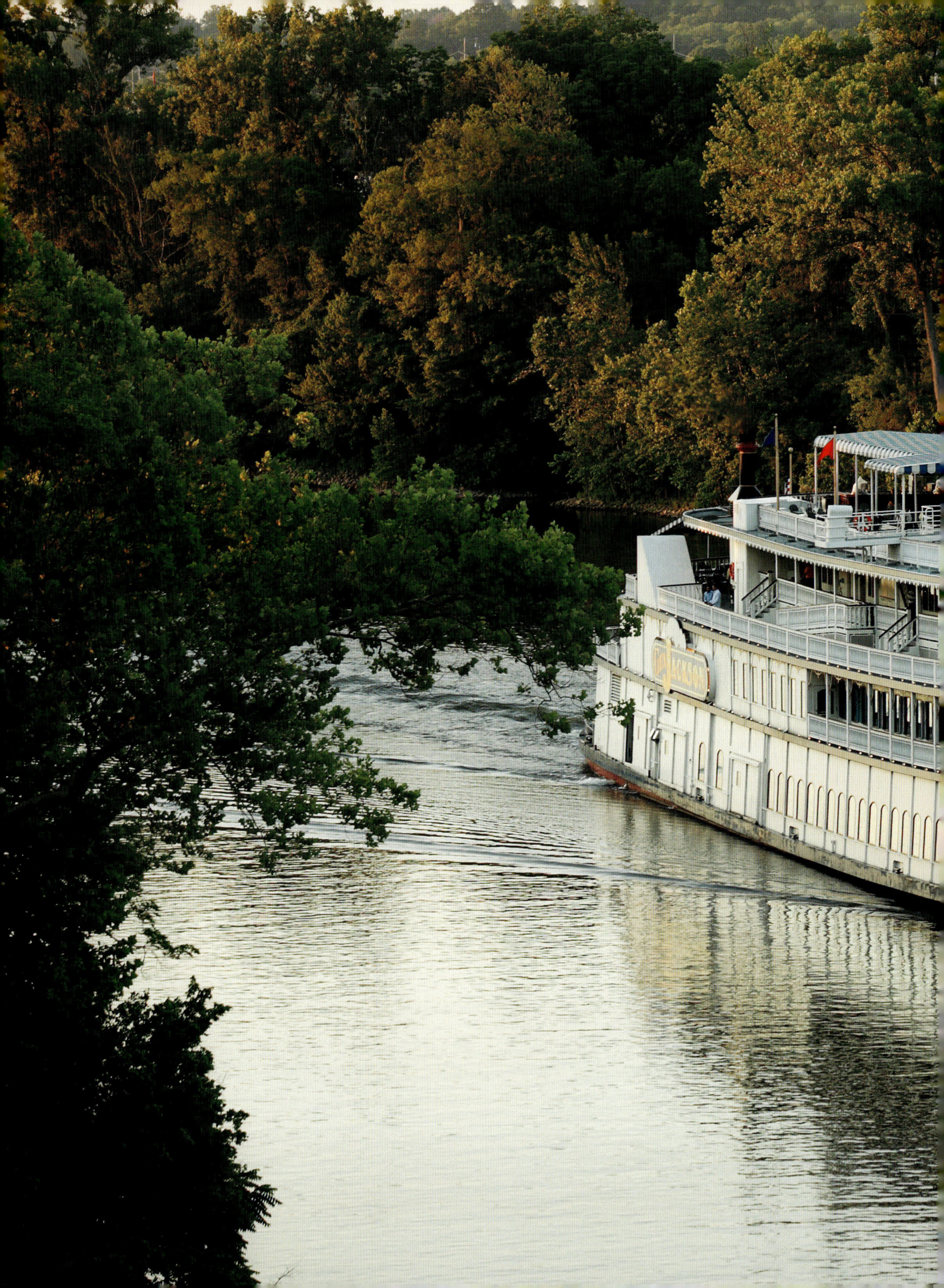

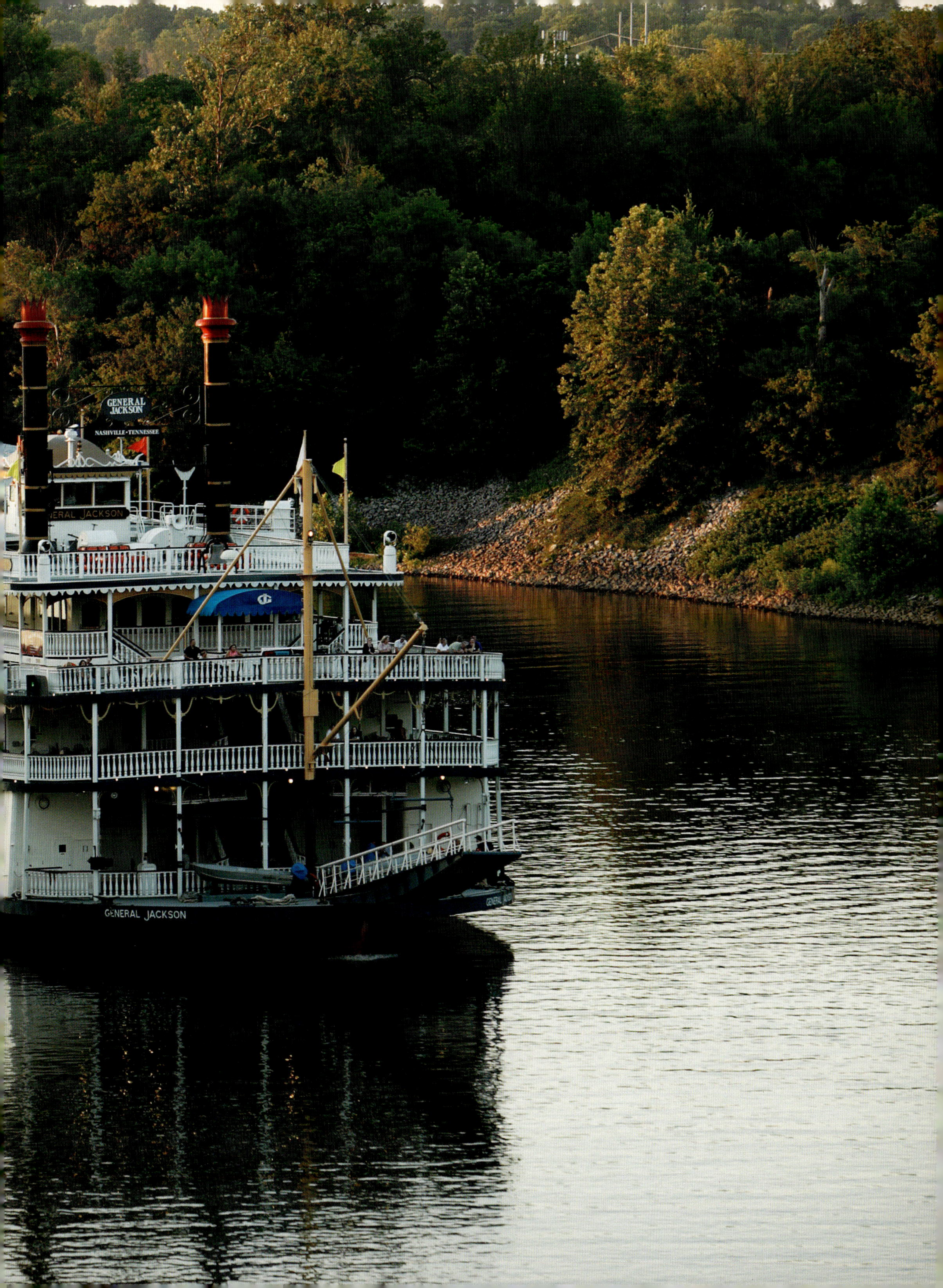
GENERAL JACKSON
NASHVILLE · TENNESSEE
GENERAL JACKSON

River Barge

The Cumberland River continues to be a vital waterway for the transportation of goods, much as it was in earlier times, when Nashville was founded along its shores. Barges move coal and other cargo up and down the river daily, to the delight of downtown visitors and workers who stop to watch them.

Radnor Lake

Radnor Lake was formed when the L&N Railroad Company purchased 1,000 acres in the Overton Hills area of Nashville in 1913 to create a water supply for its steam engines. In 1973, the threat of development led to the creation of the state's first protected area, including 747 acres.

Tennessee Agricultural Museum *(top and bottom)*

The Tennessee Agricultural Museum keeps the state's farming traditions alive, with an extensive collection of home and farm artifacts from the 19th and early 20th centuries. The museum's large farm implements, including a McCormick reaper and Jumbo steam engine, are kept in a renovated plantation barn on the grounds.

Along with farm equipment, the Tennessee Agricultural Museum has a large collection of rural Tennessee prints and folk-art sculptures. The complex also showcases a woodworking collection and other examples of arts and crafts from the state's early farming days, as well as offering demonstrations and educational programs.

Log Cabin *(opposite)*

The Tennessee Agricultural Museum's self-guided tour includes not only a stroll through the museum's collections, but also a walk throughout the grounds of the Ellington Agricultural Center. The museum maintains log cabins, a small farmhouse, a kitchen/herb garden, a perennial garden, and a nature trail.

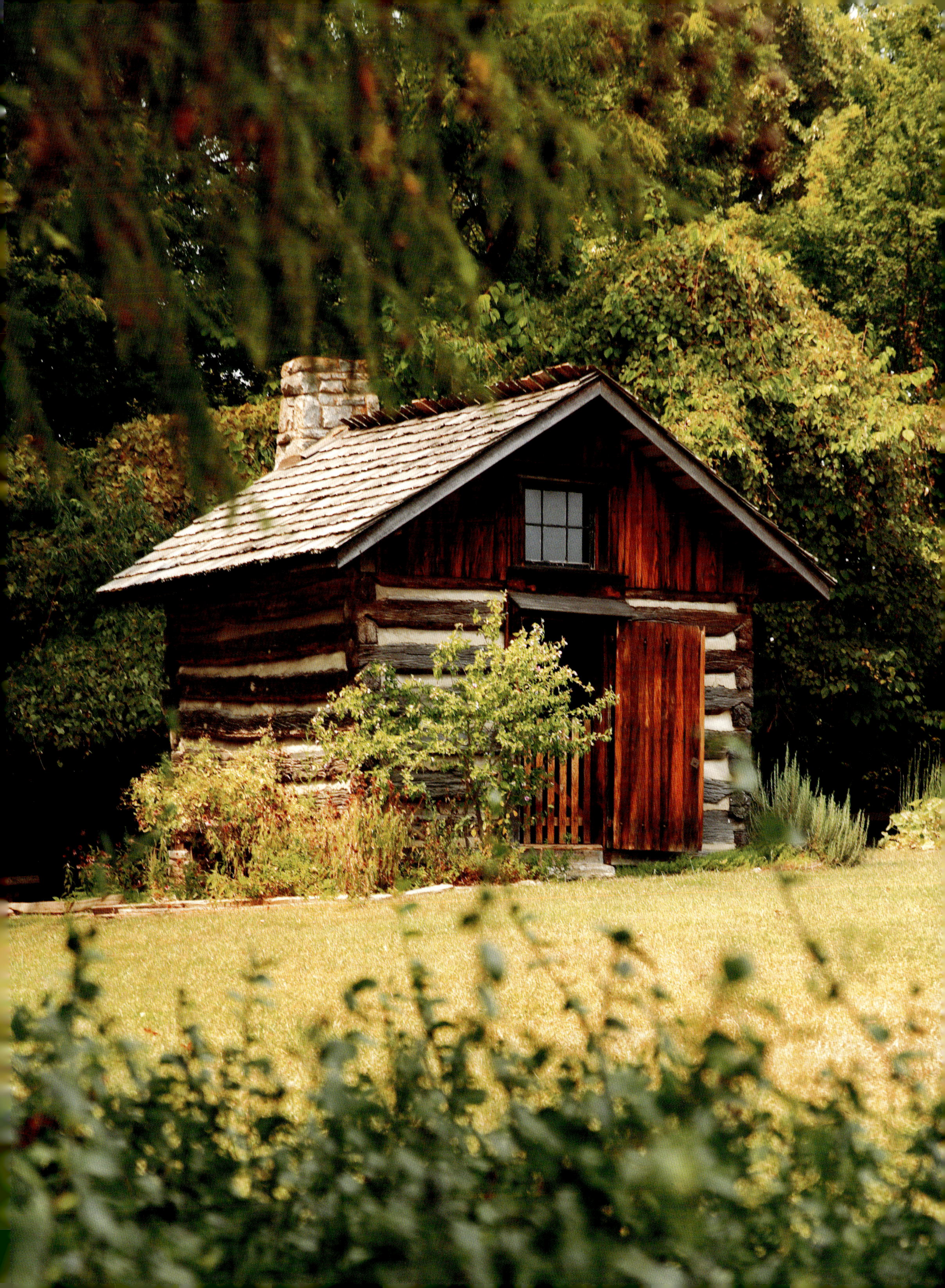

George A. Dickle Distillery

Nestled back in Cascade Hollow, on the Cumberland Plateau, the George A. Dickel distillery has been producing Tennessee Whiskey since 1870. Mr. Dickel used the nearby Cascade Springs to distill his first bottle. Dickel is the only Tennessee Whiskey that is chilled before it begins the charcoal-mellowing process.

Nashville Farmers' Market

Downtown Nashville has had a Farmers' Market since the early 1800s. The current incarnation opened in 1996, and is adjacent to the Bicentennial Mall State Park, behind the capitol building. In addition to outdoor sheds where farmers sell produce, the market also offers an indoor area with shops and restaurants.

Railroad History

Railroad history is presented in small-scale fashion at the Tennessee Central Railway Museum, housed in the former Tennessee Central Railway's master mechanic's office near downtown Nashville. The museum has amassed the largest collection of Tennessee Central Railway artifacts anywhere in addition to its growing assortment of rail cars and equipment.

Tennessee Central Railway

Railroad buffs can lose themselves for hours studying the array of exhibits at the Tennessee Central Railway Museum. The museum is devoted to chronicling and preserving the state's railroad heritage. In addition to housing historic railway equipment, the volunteer-operated museum also conducts passenger excursions in and around Middle Tennessee.

Live Theatre

The good times and good food have been rolling at Chaffin's Barn Dinner Theatre since 1967, when the Nashville landmark began staging Broadway-style musicals, comedies and more. Shows are presented year-round on the Mainstage, while the Backstage is up and running part time. Both offer the Barn's legendary buffet.

Chaffin's Barn Dinner Theatre

Nashville theatergoers have been flocking for decades to Chaffin's Barn Dinner Theatre in anticipation of a terrific Southern-style buffet and a big-city stage production featuring the best of local singers and actors; they're never disappointed. Chaffin's Barn is Nashville's first professional theatre with a variety of comedies, musicals and mysteries performed throughout the year.

Gaylord Opryland Resort *(above)*

With 2,881 guest rooms and more than 600,000 square feet of meeting space, the Gaylord Opryland Resort & Convention Center is a city unto itself. The hotel's glass-domed interior features nine acres of tropical splendor, with lush vegetation, trees, and towering water features maintained year-round by a squadron of trained groundskeepers.

Opryland Hotel *(opposite)*

A river really does run through it at the Gaylord Opryland Resort & Convention Center, which offers Delta flatboat tours of the property throughout the day and into the evening. The hotel's "city under a glass" reputation brings visitors from around the world to enjoy its spa, nightclubs, and other world-class amenities.

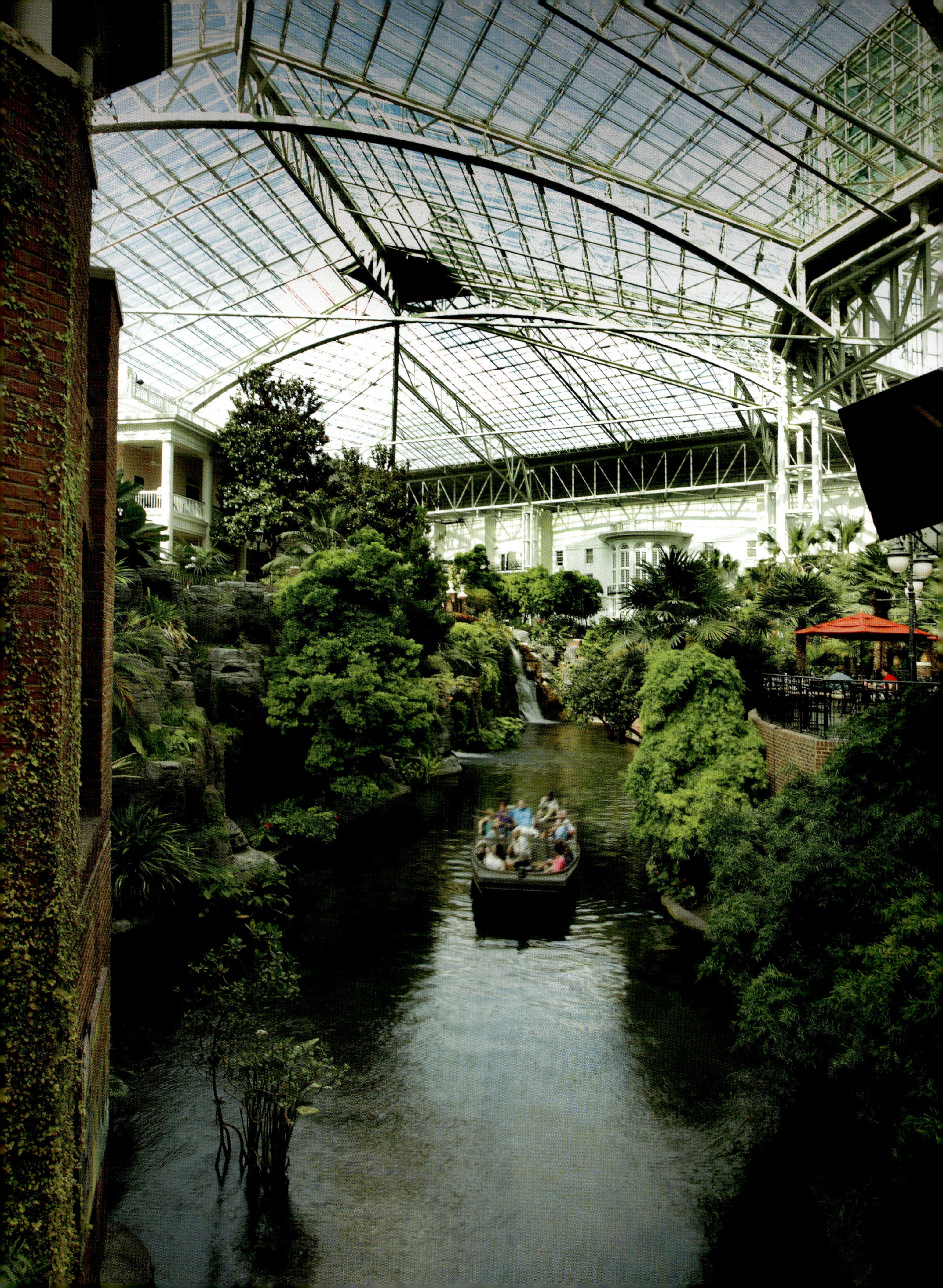

Ryman Auditorium

Captain Thomas G. Ryman opened the auditorium that bears his name in 1892 for worship services. By 1943 it had become the Mother Church of Country Music, hosting the Grand Ole Opry until 1974. The Ryman still rocks, routinely selling out for top-name touring musicians and entertainers.

Grand Ole Opry House

Since 1974, the Grand Ole Opry has broadcast its radio and television shows from this location, built on a former farm site in the Pennington Bend of the Cumberland River. The 4,400-seat Grand Ole Opry House hosts the show year-round, except for a brief annual winter run at the Ryman Auditorium in downtown Nashville.

Music Row *(top and bottom)*

Some eyebrows were raised at the unveiling of *Musica* in 2003, but the statue, which anchors the northern end of Music Row in the center of a roundabout, has proven to be popular with locals and tourists alike. Many will often circle it several times to get just the right photograph.

Legendary musicians have made their name on Music Row for decades, and some have left a more permanent mark. A few have even been honored with their own piece of roadway. The offices and converted homes along these streets, as well as Music Row itself, are the vibrant face of the country-music industry.

Gaylord Entertainment

Gaylord Entertainment is one of many companies doing a brisk business on Music Row. Country-music promoters, publicists and related industry professionals jostle for signage and street space at the epicenter of the famous Nashville-based industry, where recording studios and more than a few future stars can be found.

Owen Bradley (above)

Near the north end of Music Row stands the Owen Bradley Park, a lasting tribute to the famed songwriter, performer, and publisher whose list of contributions to both country music and performers are beyond legendary. This statue shows Bradley at one of his favorite spots, behind a piano.

Music Publishing (opposite)

Sony/ATV Tree Music Publishing is one of many publishing houses on Music Row. Sony has been a haven for writers who crank out stories of heartache, desertion, new love, and other major life events. These stories eventually find their way onto paper, into the recording studio, and out onto the airwaves.

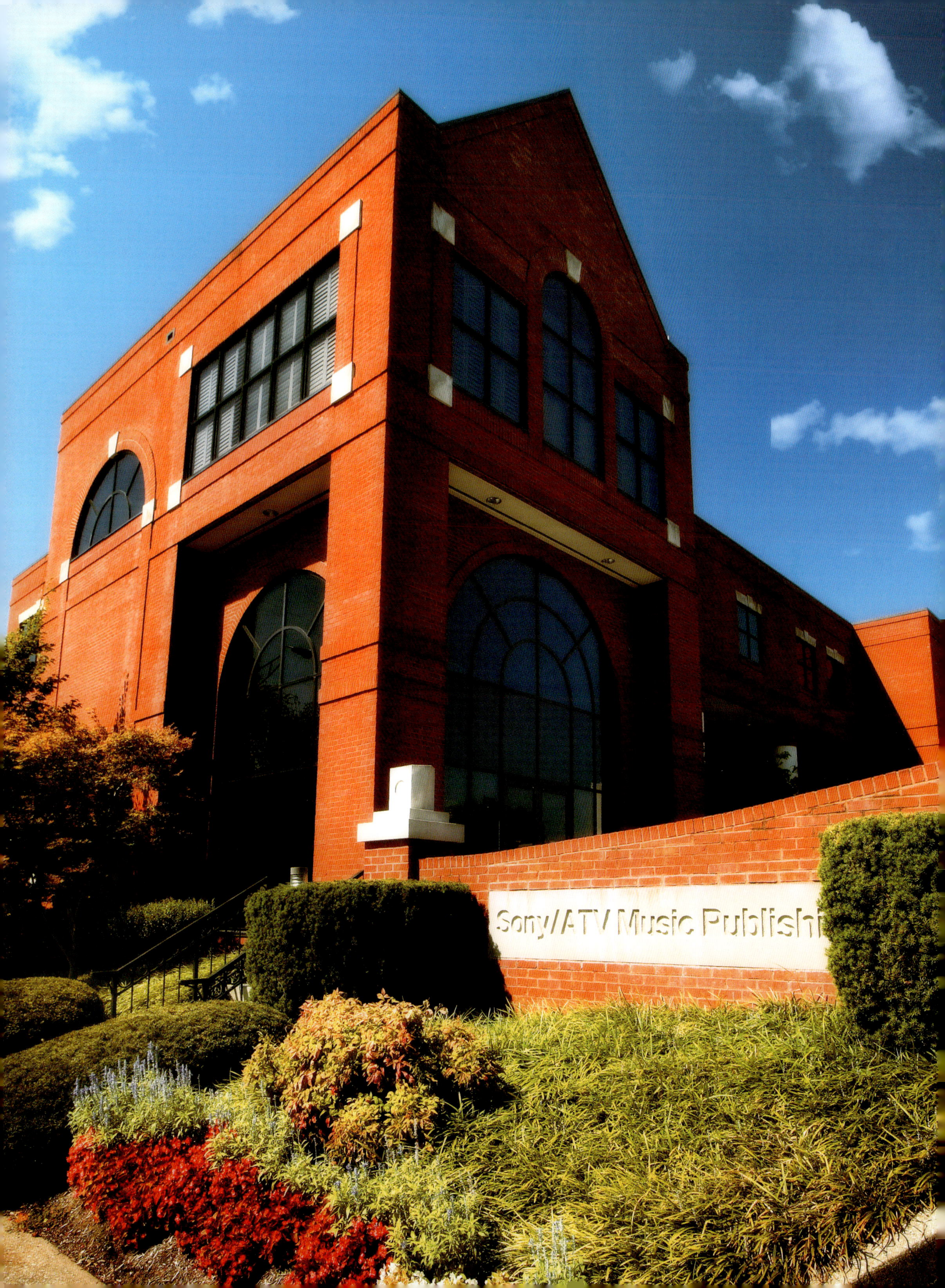
Sony/ATV Music Publishi

Musicians Hall of Fame (top and bottom)

The Musicians Hall of Fame & Museum is dedicated to the artists who created some of the world's best-known recordings. A walk through the exhibit hall turns up some famous faces, as well as plenty of lesser-known artists who, nonetheless, made great contributions to the industry.

Drummer Hal Blaine

The Musicians Hall of Fame & Museum features instruments mastered by honorees of many classic recordings. Although session drummer Hal Blaine's name may not be famous, he has played on hundreds of hit records recognizable around the world. The museum is continually adding to its collection.

Wurlitzer Jutebox *(above and left)*

Visitors to the Musicians Hall of Fame & Museum are immersed in the sights and sounds of several decades' worth of hits. The hall of fame's members have played on thousands of instantly recognizable recordings found not only on this classic-style jukebox, but are still heard on the radio today.

Historic RCA Studio B *(above and right)*

At RCA Studio B, fans can get an upclose glimpse inside the studio where their favorite music legends recorded some of the most memorable hits. Elvis Presley, Chet Atkins, and the Everly Brothers are just a few of the notable artists that crooned at the studio, which now is a learning laboratory for nearby Belmont University.

Music Valley Wax Museum *(top and bottom)*

A plethora of country-music legends are immortalized at the Music Valley Wax Museum. The museum has over 50 life-sized figures dressed in authentic costumes. While the collection includes artists from the legendary Kitty Wells to contemporary favorite Alan Jackson, they're always awaiting the next big star.

The "Sidewalk of the Stars" outside the Music Valley Wax Museum includes the lasting impressions of more than 300 of country music's most famous stars. Reconizable artists who have left their mark include Loretta Lynn, Porter Wagoner, and Randy Travis.

Robert's Western World *(top and bottom)*

Robert's Western World in Nashville's Lower Broadway music district offers both fine Western wear as well as excellent live musical entertainment. In addition, a menu that includes fried bologna and pork-chop sandwiches earns it the international reputation of "honky-tonk with a difference."

Country Music Hall of Fame *(top and bottom)*

Since 1967, music fans from around the world have paid homage to many stars at the Country Music Hall of Fame and Museum, which opened its new downtown Nashville building in May 2001. In addition to thousands of artifacts on display, the building's rotunda offers a cathedral-like setting for the legends enshrined there.

Ernest Tubb Record Shop *(opposite)*

For more than 50 years, the Ernest Tubb Record Shop has done a brisk business in country, gospel, and bluegrass recordings. *The Ernest Tubb Midnight Jamboree*, a live radio show following the Grand Ole Opry, broadcasts directly from the shop, which is also home to The Green Hornet, Tubb's famous tour bus.

ERNEST TUBB

1914 – 1984

Dedicated To His Many
Fans With Our Thanks
And Gratitude On The
40th Anniversary Of
Ernest Tubb Record Shop
May 3, 1987

Gruhn Guitars *(left and right)*

Since its opening in 1970 in downtown Nashville, Gruhn Guitars has been a must-stop for serious strummers. Now, with four stories and almost 13,000 square feet of space, the famed Gruhn continues to provide both new and vintage guitars, as well as painstaking repair and restoration work for customers worldwide.

Willie Nelson & Family General Store

It may not be the best stop for groceries, but Willie Nelson & Friends General Store & Museum offers plenty of choice merchandise. Since 1979, wares have included displays of star photos as well as plenty of Willie's own memorabilia. The store has also hosted special events, book signings, and live performances.

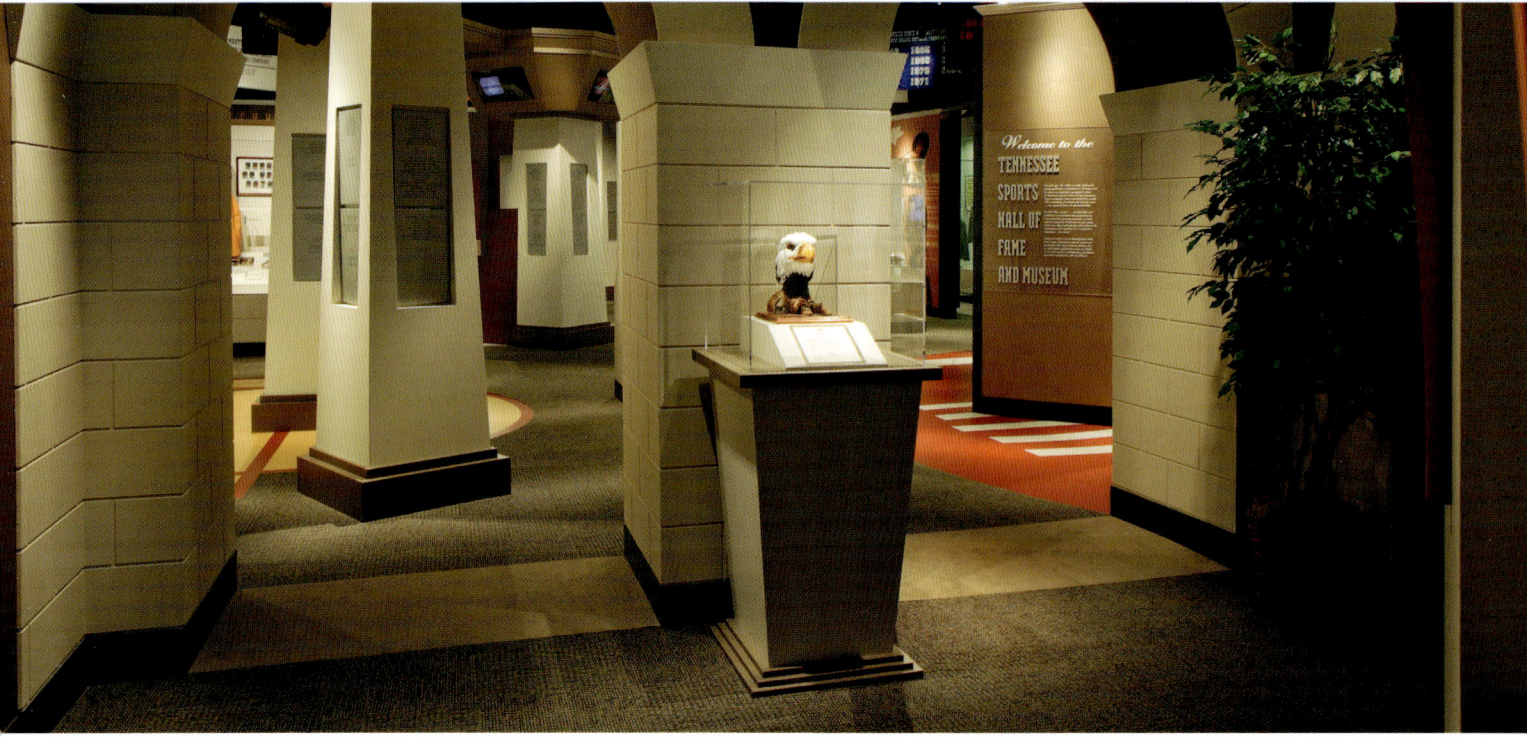

Tennessee Sports Hall of Fame *(top and bottom)*

The Tennessee Sports Hall of Fame was organized by the Middle Tennessee Sportswriters and Broadcasters Association in the 1960s, and was officially created by an act of the state legislature in 1994. Since its inception, the Hall of Fame's annual induction dinner has been a "who's who" of Tennessee sports legends.

The Tennessee Sports Hall of Fame and its 7,200-square-foot, interactive museum are housed on the main level of The Sommet Center. Visitors can play a virtual-reality, one-on-one basketball game, try their hand at strength-training equipment used by Olympic swimmers, and enjoy sports videos in two 30-seat theaters.

The Upper Room Ministries

More than 10,000 people visit the Upper Room headquarters each year to see the Upper Room Chapel, and the famous woodcarving of Da Vinci's *The Last Supper* sculpted by Ernest Pellegrini. The museum contains a collection reflecting the Upper Room's international, interracial, and interdenominational nature.

Tennessee Walking Horse Museum
(top and bottom)

Equestrian enthusiasts keep the turnstiles busy at the Tennessee Walking Horse Museum, the only institution of its kind devoted solely to preserving the history of these magnificent animals. The Lynchburg facility features exhibits on the formation of the breed registry and bloodlines, as well as informative videos and other interesting displays.

Lane Motor Museum *(top and bottom)*

The Lane Motor Museum attracts enthusiasts with an appreciation for automobiles of all shapes and sizes. European cars are a specialty at the museum, which works to keep all its vehicles in perfect running order. Housed in the former Sunbeam Bakery, the museum also includes an exhibit that honors the building's history.

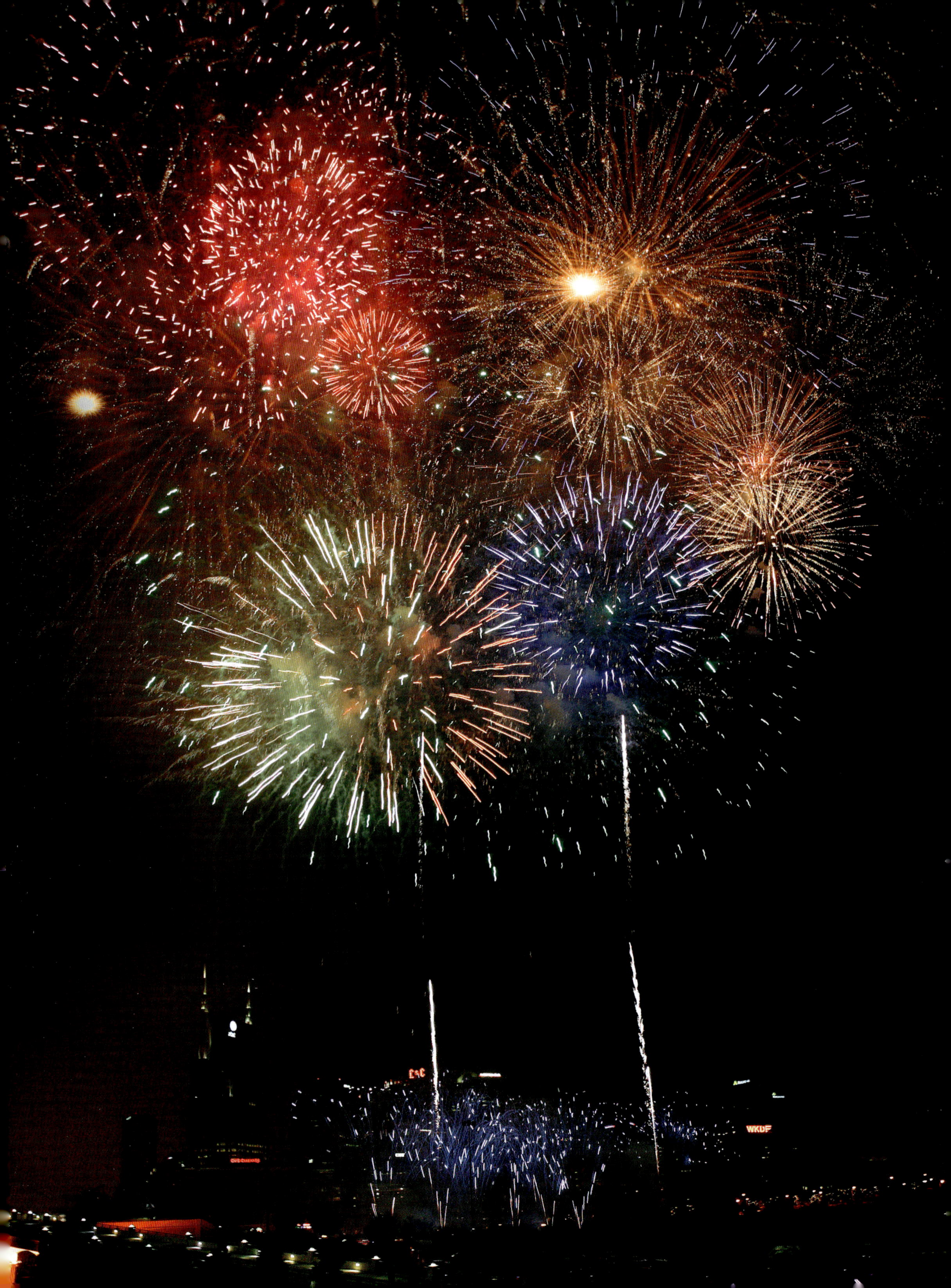
WKDF

Fourth of July *(opposite)*

Downtown Nashville comes alive on the Fourth of July, when Riverfront Park is packed with music lovers who eagerly await the Nashville Symphony's annual outdoor concert. Each Independence Day, the city of Nashville puts on the largest fireworks display in the South, choreographed in tune with the symphony's patriotic selections.

Schermerhorn Symphony Center *(top)*

The Schermerhorn Symphony Center has been hailed as a major addition to the classical music world. Opened in 2006, the center's rich acoustics bring out the best in both vocal and instrumental performers. Inspired by great European concert halls, the exterior features nine granite and limestone fountains, including the Harmony Fountain and its 15-foot, bronze sculpture, *The Birth of Apollo.*

The Nashville Symphony *(bottom)*

The Nashville Symphony is reknowned worldwide for its live performances as well as its Grammy-winning recordings. From 1920 to present, the symphony has flourished, rising to new heights under the baton of the late Maestro Kenneth Schermerhorn. The symphony has performed at New York's prestigious Carnegie Hall.

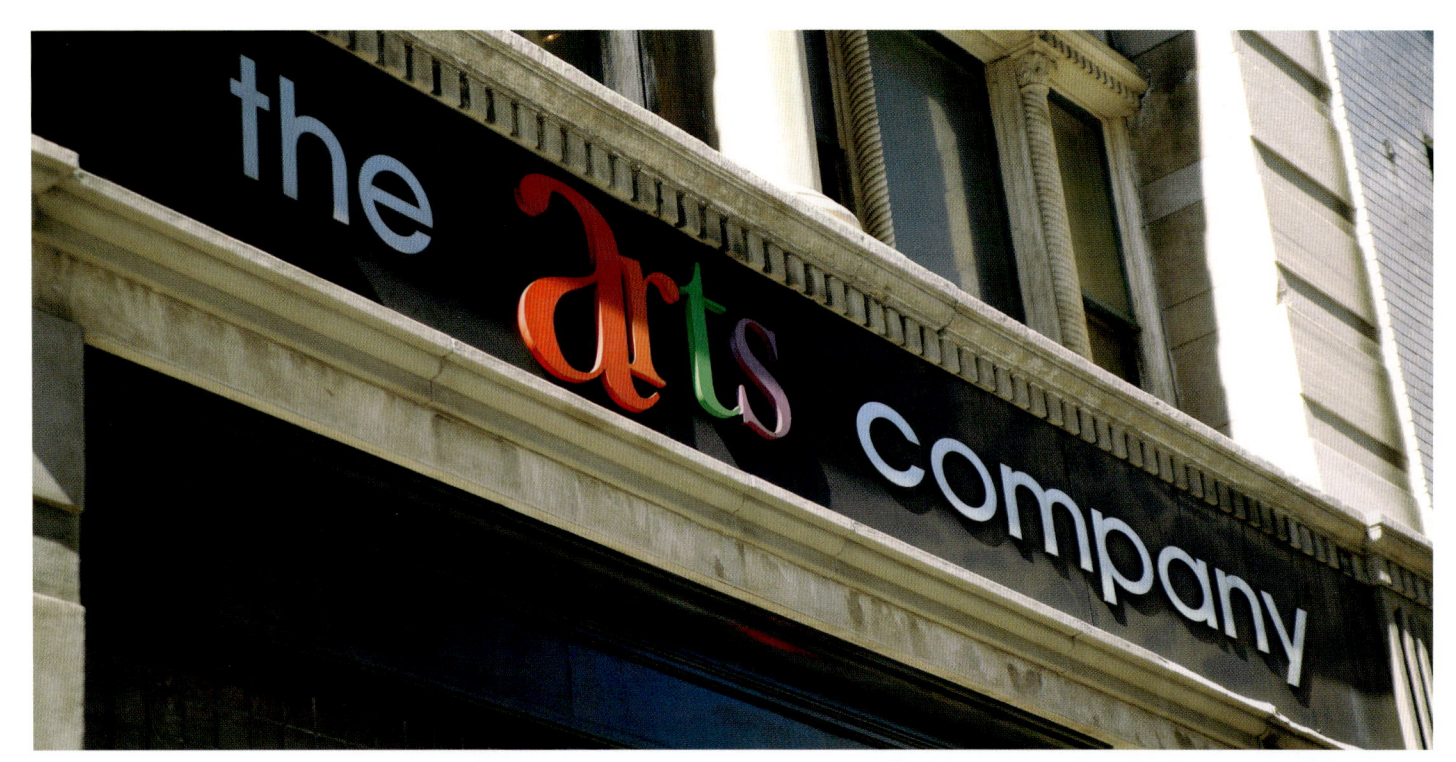

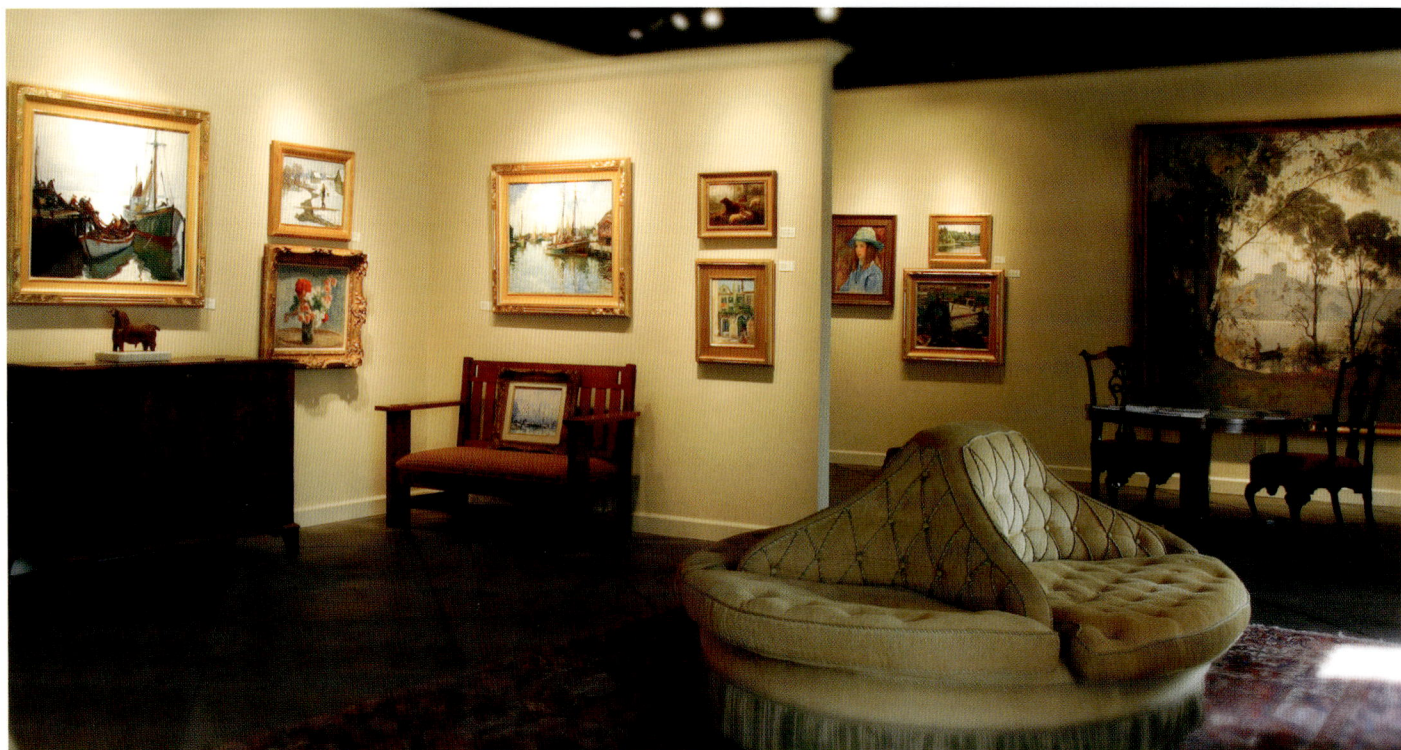

The Arts Company (top)

Since opening in 1996, The Arts Company has been a leader in Nashville's fine arts community. The gallery showcases photography, painting, and sculpture by both new and established artists. Up and coming talent is featured each month during its "First Art Saturdays," held in more than 6,000 square feet of space in downtown Nashville.

Stanford Art Gallery (bottom)

The Stanford Art Gallery houses a well-known collection of Impressionist paintings by 19th and 20th-century American and European artists. The gallery's offerings represent those of highly-collectible artists, making it a frequent stop for serious fine-art collectors.

The Rymer Gallery

One of the newest players on the Nashville art scene is the Rymer Gallery, which showcases contemporary art from both emerging and established artists who work in a variety of mediums. Located near the large gallery is an annex gallery, as well as an artist's studio. The Rymer Gallery strives to promote the best in modern works from Nashville's vibrant arts community.

Union Station

Now a Wyndham Historic Hotel, Nashville's Union Station stands as a lasting tribute to the golden age of railroad travel. The heavy, stone building, constructed in the Richardsonian-Romanesque style, opened in 1900, and is well known for its 65-foot, barrel-vaulted, lobby ceiling that features gold-leaf medallions and 100-year-old, original Luminous Prism stained glass.

Wyndham Historic Hotel

The lofty turrets and towers of Union Station have withstood more than a century of change in downtown Nashville. The impressive building is still a hub of activity in its current luxury-hotel incarnation. It was designated a National Historic Landmark in 1977, and was rededicated in 2007, following an 11-million-dollar renovation.

Frist Center for the Visual Arts

Nashville's art deco post office took on a new role in 2001, reopening as the Frist Center for the Visual Arts. With rotating exhibitions every six to eight weeks, the Frist prides itself on an ever-changing, unique rosters, as well as popular children's programs in the Martin ArtQuest Gallery.

Financial District

Nashville has long been a financial hub of the South. As locally-founded banks give way to regional and national giants, the industry still maintains a strong presence in the city's center. Many of Nashville's skyscrapers bear the names of some of the country's best-known financial institutions.

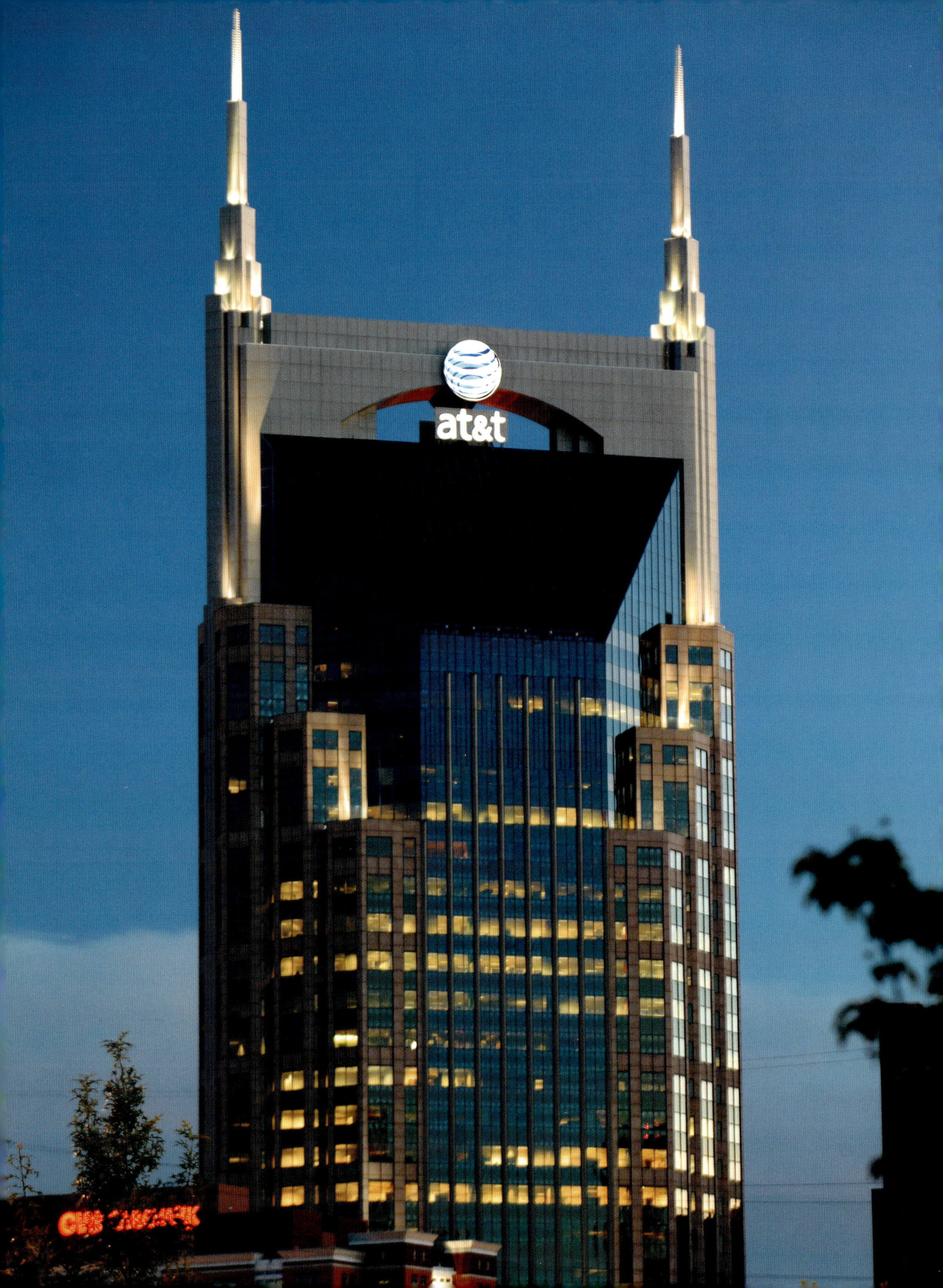
at&t

The Batman Building (opposite)

The AT&T Building became a fixture on the Nashville skyline even before the construction cranes came down. Completed in 1994, it is currently the tallest building in the state of Tennessee. The 32-story skyscraper has a capacity of up to 2,000 workers. It aquired its nickname, "The Batman Building," almost immediately after opening.

Lower Broadway (above)

The soul of Music City resonates in the shops, restaurants, and honky-tonks of Lower Broadway, an area rich in country-music history. Performers from the Grand Ole Opry often mix it up with starry-eyed newcomers and house bands from legendary clubs such as Tootsie's Orchid Lounge.

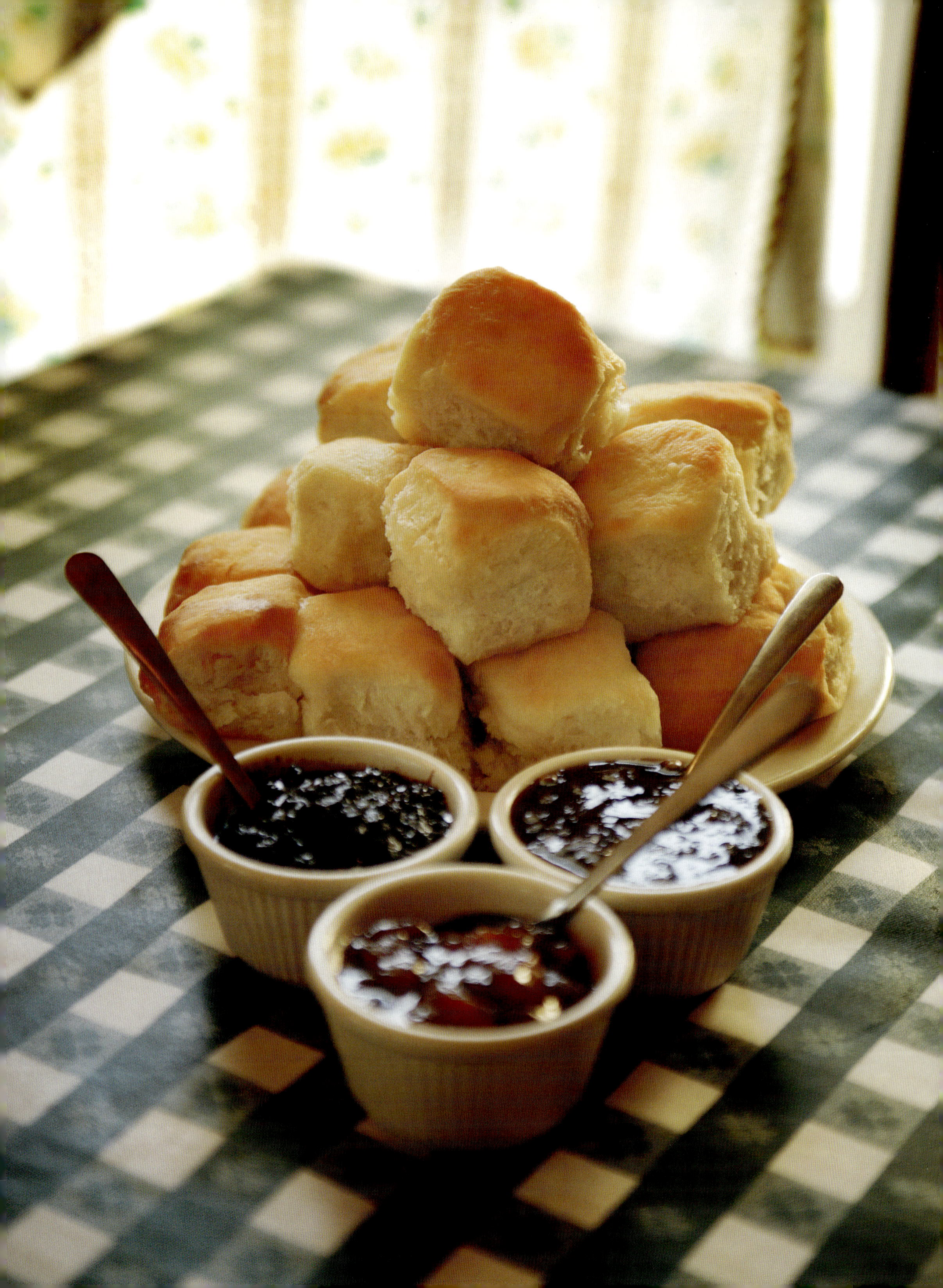

Loveless Café *(opposite and above)*

Located out on Highway 100, near the northern end of the Natchez Trace Parkway, the Loveless Café offers up some serious southern hospitality. Once a motel and café, the Loveless is now devoted, full-time, to serving its famous fried chicken and biscuits, as well as selling delicious preserves and other homemade goodies.

WILDHORSE
SALOON
Wildhorse Store
Get Your Concert
Tickets Here
OPEN

Wildhorse Saloon *(opposite)*

Downtown Nashville, a sometimes rowdy riverfront strip, features the lively Wildhorse Saloon. This historic, three-story warehouse is home to one of the city's most popular restaurant and nightclub venues, presenting top-name country stars in concert. Approximately 1.5 million people visit the Wildhorse each year.

Hard Rock Café *(top)*

The Hard Rock Café is well suited alongside all the other country-music venues in Lower Broadway. The Hard Rock performed a civic service of sorts when it opened in 1994, gentrifying the site that allegedly housed Nashville's first brothel.

Hermitage Hotel *(bottom)*

When it opened in 1908, the Hermitage Hotel advertised its rooms as "fireproof, noiseproof, and dustproof," however, it was the luxurious interior that has drawn presidents and dignitaries over the decades. Lovingly renovated, the Hermitage reopened in 2000, and is still the last word in downtown elegance.

Printer's Alley (top and bottom)

Named for its proximity to the city's printing and publishing industry in the mid-20th century, Printer's Alley offers revelers a variety of venues. The alley is best known for its lively nightlife, which offers up a little bit of Bourbon Street in the heart of downtown Nashville.

Hatch Show Print (opposite)

The unique woodblock posters and handbills created at Hatch Show Print have become famous the world over, ever since Charles R. and Herbert H. Hatch began turning their presses in 1879. Now owned and operated by the Country Music Foundation, Hatch's unique works of art continue to advertise coming attractions and more.

ACE OF CLUBS
THE SEXTANTS
CONCERT FOR MANGLERDESH
MON. OCT. 19
GUITAR GABRIEL
ANTIQUE
JULY 29 30 31
LIVE
QUEEN ELIZABETH HALL

Nashville Visitors Center

To get the most out of a great Music City vacation, many tourists start downtown at the Visitor Information Center. Equipped with everything from maps and brochures, to tickets, show times, and copies of the collectible Music City Hits CD, staffers pride themselves in providing all the details to create informative and customized outings.

Shelby Street Pedestrian Bridge

The Shelby Street Bridge has carried Nashville's traffic across the Cumberland River since 1909. It was the first bridge in North America to have concrete arched trusses, and was appointed to the National Register of Historic Places in 1998. After restoration work, it was reopened as a pedestrian bridge in 2003.

Nashville Superspeedway

The Nashville Superspeedway has been bringing racing excitement to Middle Tennessee since 2001. Built by Dover Motorsports in Lebanon, the 1.33-mile, fully lit, D-shaped concrete track hosts NASCAR's Nationwide Series and Camping World Truck Series events, as well as offering motorcycle, road course and drag-racing excitement to 150,000 fans at a time.

Centennial Sportsplex

The 17-acre Centennial Sportsplex is a year-round family fitness center that truly has something for everyone. The tennis center hosts several tournaments annually on its 15 outdoor, hard-surface tennis courts, including one with 2,500 spectator seats. The complex also offers four indoor courts and a fully stocked pro shop.

Centennial Sportsplex

The Centennial Sportsplex offers everything from exercise rooms to ice-skating. The facility acts as the practice rink for the Nashville Predators, and several amateur hockey leagues also call the Sportsplex home. A fully-stocked fitness center and diverse roster of classes, clinics, and programs round out the facility's appeal.

Aquatics Center

The aquatics center at the Centennial Sportsplex has hosted the U.S. Senior and Junior National swim meets, as well as a wide range of other events, at its competition pool. The complex also offers a smaller, recreational pool and a diving well, along with a variety of swimming and water-fitness classes.

Adventure Science Center

The Adventure Science Center has been educating Nashville's youth since 1944, when it began as the Children's Museum of Nashville. With over 260,000 visitors annually, the facility continues to offer a wide variety of fun and educational exhibits.

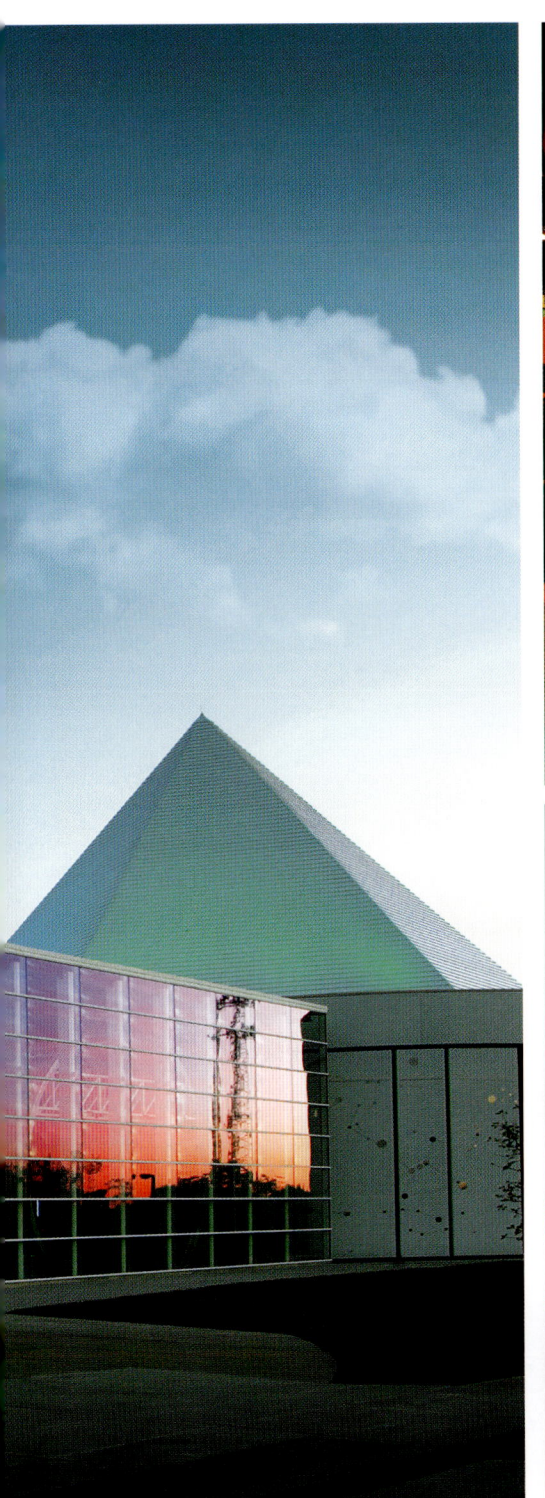

The Sky's the Limit (top and bottom)

Child-sized interactive exhibits offer many hands-on learning opportunitites to the center's young visitors, while the Sudekum Planetarium at the Adventure Science Center is a stargazer's delight. A GOTO Chiron Hybrid star projector, the first of its kind in the United States, projects 6.5 million stars on a dome that measures 63 feet in diameter, while a Digistar 3 projection system provides full-color, high-resolution imagery across the dome.

Aaron Douglas Gallery

The Aaron Douglas Gallery at Fisk University features rotating exhibitions from the university's permanent collection of African art, as well as works from Fisk's fine-arts students and faculty. The university is also home to the Alfred Stieglitz Collection of Modern Art, which contains many works by noted artist Georgia O'Keeffe.

Fisk University

Cravath Hall honors the Reverend Erastus Milo Cravath, one of Fisk University's three founders. The institution, once called the Fisk School in Nashville, opened its doors just after the end of the Civil War. The university's founders had one goal: to establish an educational institution open to all, regardless of race, with high standards of education.

Scarritt-Bennet Center

The 10 acres of the Scarritt-Bennett Center is a quiet oasis in the center of a busy city. Utilized as a conference center and retreat facility, Scarritt-Bennett's 10 Gothic-style, crab-orchard stone buildings house programs dedicated to overcoming racism and working toward justice and reconciliation on a global level.

Wightman Chapel

The Wightman Chapel at Scarritt-Bennett Center is surrounded by beautifully landscaped grounds, and is one of Nashville's most popular wedding and worship sites. Built in 1928, the Gothic-style chapel seats 300 people and has a 90-foot center aisle. It has been included on the National Register of Historic Places.

Tennessee State University *(top)*

Offering 45 bachelor's degrees, 24 master's degrees, seven doctoral programs, and a full roster of intramural athletics, Tennessee State University is a major player in Nashville's higher-education arena. The land-grant institution was founded in 1912, and is often listed in the *U.S. News & World Report*'s Guide to America's Best Colleges.

Tennessee State Museum *(bottom)*

The Tennessee State Museum occupies three floors in the James K. Polk Center in downtown Nashville. It was created in 1937 by the state's General Assembly to hold World War I artifacts and other collections, although its history dates back to 1817. The museum has 60,000 square feet of space devoted to exhibits.

Vanderbilt University *(opposite)*

Commodore Cornelius Vanderbilt envisioned an institute of higher learning that would bind all sections of the country together, and in 1873 he donated one million dollars to make that happen. The resulting institution, Vanderbilt University, is now one of the world's top research facilities and an internationally-recognized educational center.

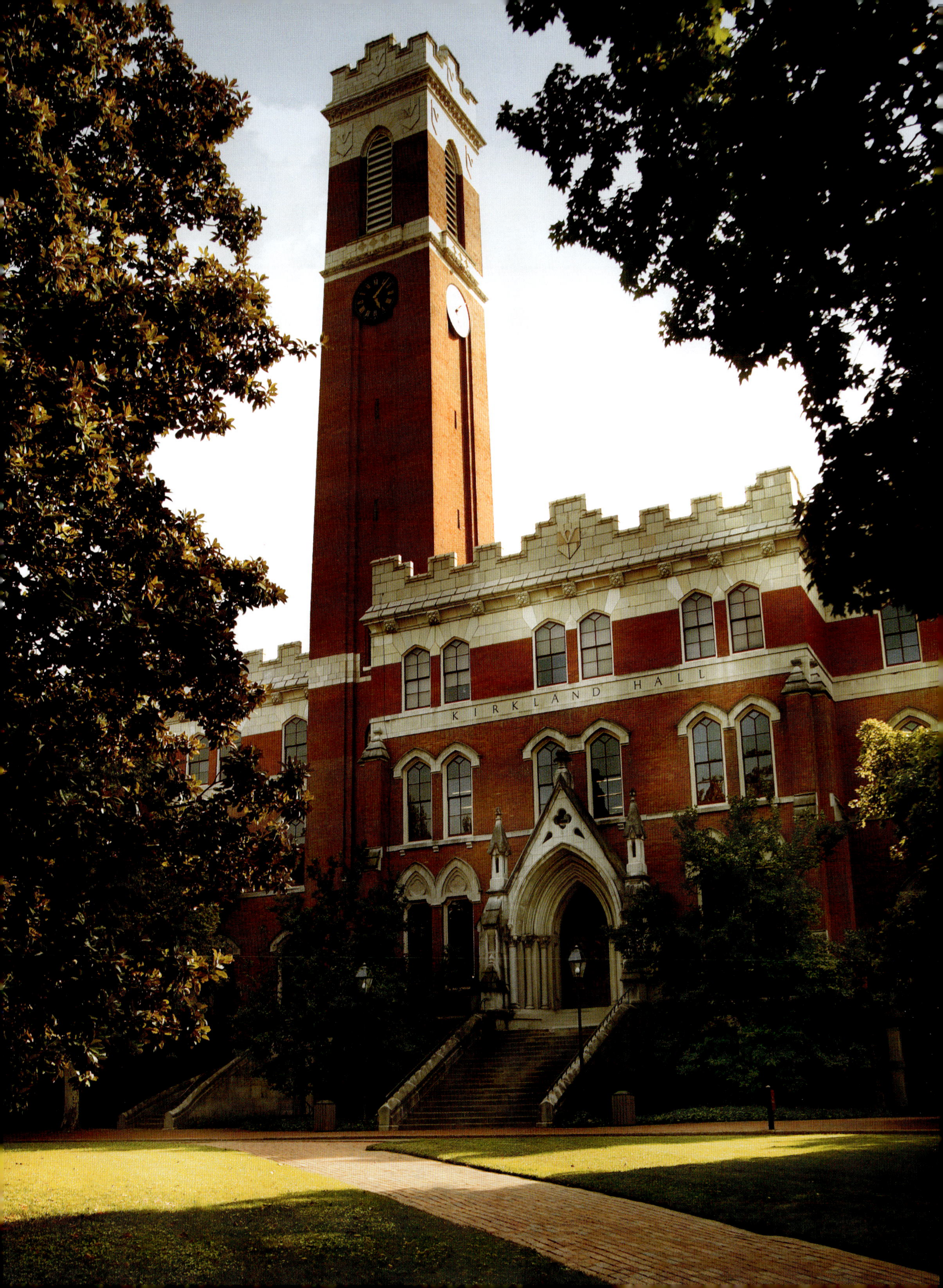
KIRKLAND HALL

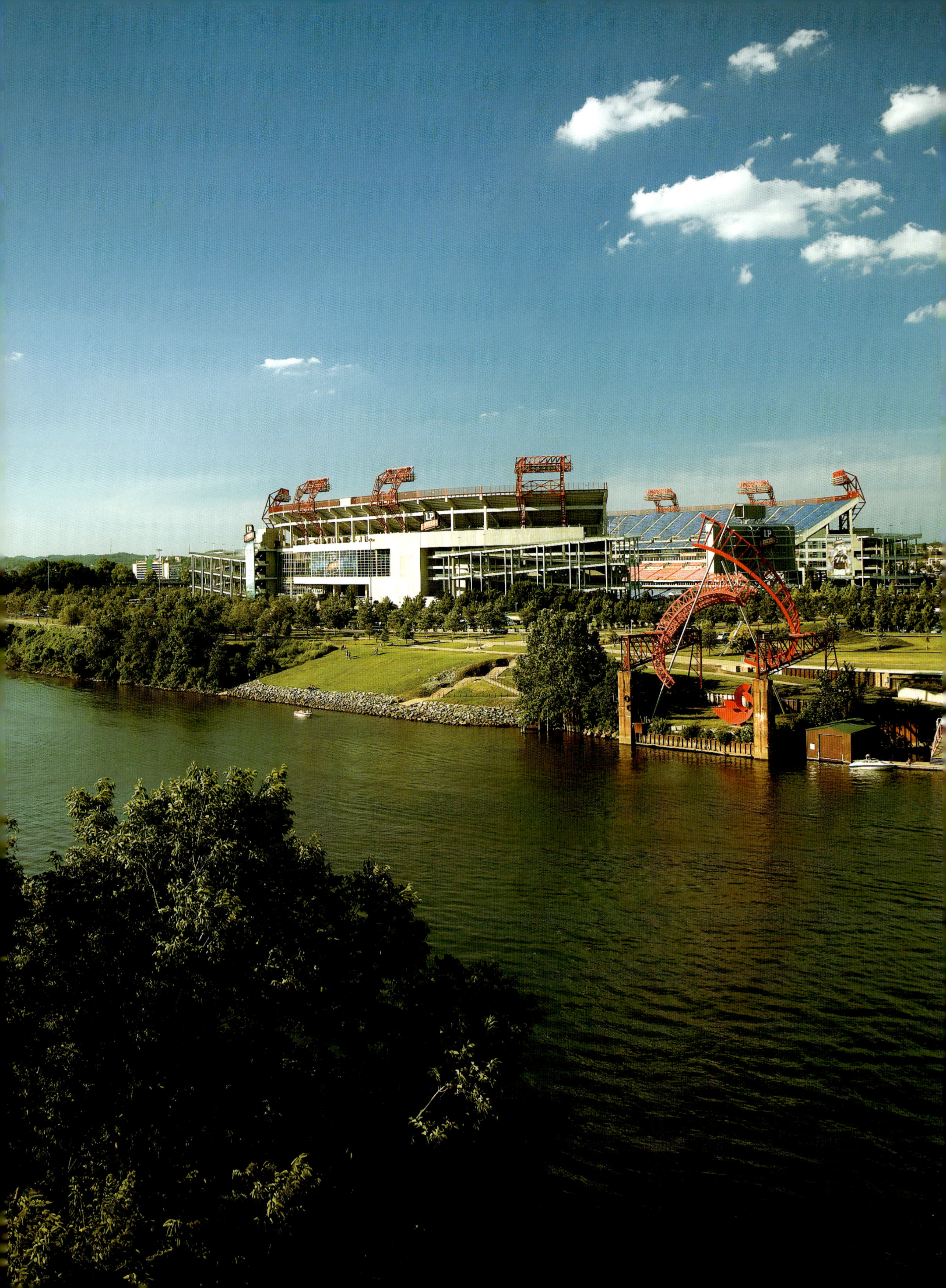

LP Field *(opposite and top)*

When the Houston Oilers came to town as the Tennessee Titans in 1997, LP Field™ was waiting for them. Known previously as Adelphia Coliseum, the new facility on the banks of the Cumberland River survived a major tornado during its construction. It hosted the first Titans game in 1999.

The Tennessee Titans have made LP Field™ one of the best-known sports venues in the Southeast. The stadium holds 68,798 fans and routinely rocks on home-game Sundays. The telecast of the occasional Monday Night Football game takes the field, and the city, to living rooms around the country.

Nashville Sounds *(bottom)*

The Pacific Coast League Nashville Sounds are the Triple-A affiliate of the Milwaukee Brewers, and play their home games at Herschel Greer Stadium. The team was established at the Double-A level in 1978, and then moved to the Triple-A level in 1985. It has served as a farm club for six major-league franchises.

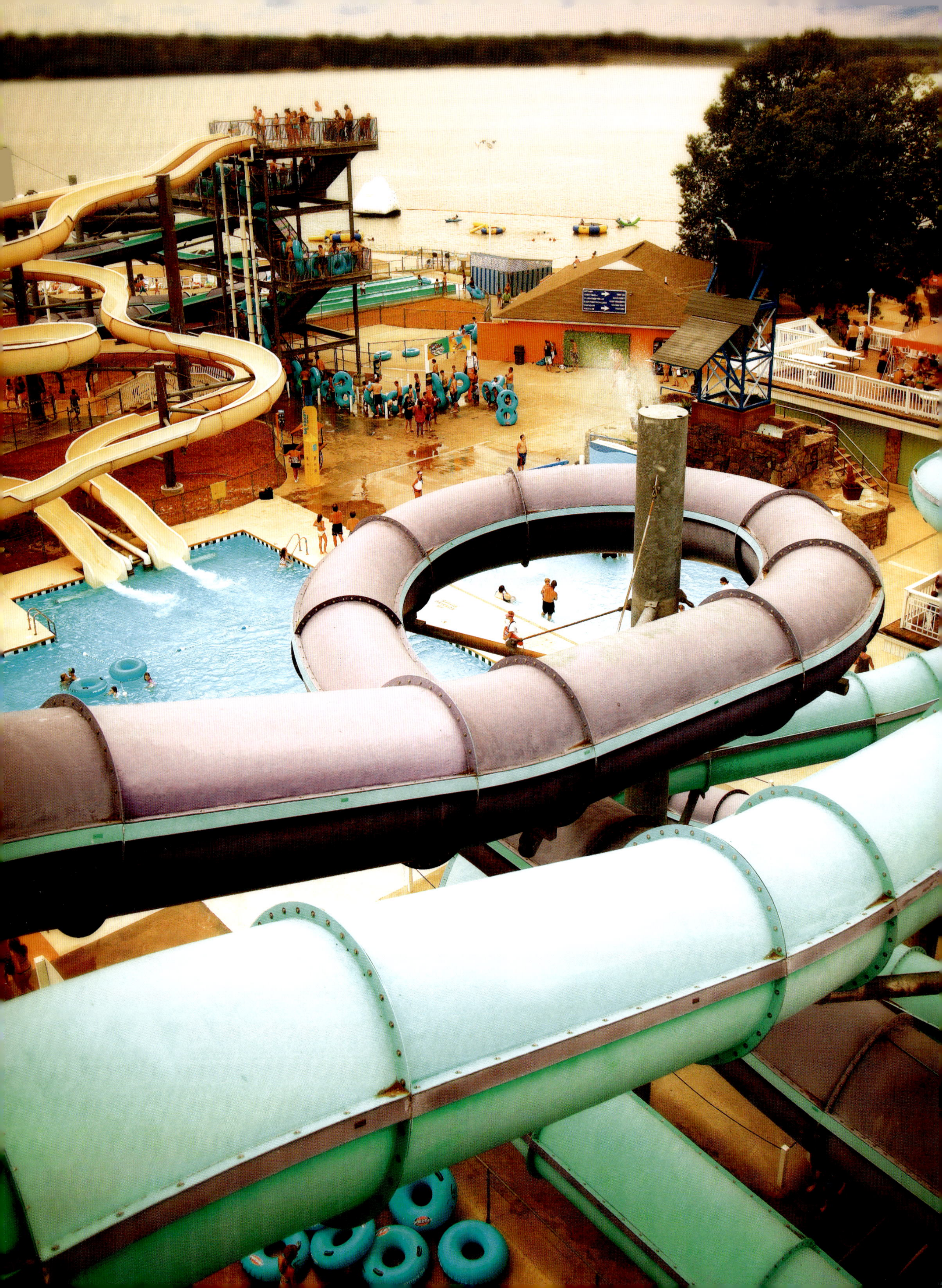

Nashville Shores (opposite and above)

Splashing down at Nashville Shores is one of Nashvillians' favorite summertime activities. The facility sports a beach along J. Percy Priest Lake, as well as large and kid-sized pools, water slides, and more. For those who want to venture out on the lake, pontoon boats and other watercraft are available for rent.

Nashville Shores offers family fun during the scorching days of a Middle Tennessee summer. It's also one of the area's most popular spots for business meetings, family reunions, and graduation parties due to its proximity to J. Percy Priest Lake, one of the areas most widely-visited boating and fishing spots.

David Bailey

Since 1994, David Bailey Photography has represented some of the country's most highly recognized corporations and media outlets, including *Time Magazine*, Wells Fargo, Legg Mason, Jack Daniels, Johnston & Murphy, Bridgestone/Firestone, Exxon, Dell Computer, and Tractor Supply Co.

David has more than 20 years' experience; evident in his ability to artistically capture the spirit of each image with a genuine depth of emotion. His award-winning work has come from both client assignments and self-assigned projects that are included in his portfolio of stock photography.

In addition to his work in and around Nashville, David has traveled the United States and the world, in search of moments waiting to be forever captured on a photographic journey. To see more of David's work, visit www.davidbaileyphotography.com.

Joe Morris is a Nashville-based writer and editor. His career has spanned from small-town newspaper work in South Carolina to celebrity interviews in Los Angeles, and just about everything in between. He currently writes about local government, tourism and hospitality, legal affairs, health care, and other subjects for local, regional, and national print and online publications.